Gay, Lesbian, Bisexual, Transgender and Questioning Teen Literature

Genreflecting Advisory Series

Diana Tixier Herald, Series Editor

Graphic Novels: A Genre Guide to Comic Books, Manga, and More
Michael Pawuk

Genrefied Classics: A Guide to Reading Interests in Classic Literature
Tina Frolund

Encountering Enchantment: A Guide to Speculative Fiction for Teens
Susan Fichtelberg

Fluent in Fantasy: The Next Generation
Diana Tixier Herald and Bonnie Kunzel

Gay, Lesbian, Bisexual, and Transgendered Literature: A Genre Guide
Ellen Bosman and John Bradford; Edited by Robert B. Ridinger

Reality Rules!: A Guide to Teen Nonfiction Reading Interest
Elizabeth Fraser

Historical Fiction II: A Guide to the Genre
Sarah L. Johnson

Hooked on Horror III
Anthony J. Fonseca and June Michele Pulliam

Caught Up in Crime: A Reader's Guide to Crime Fiction and Nonfiction
Gary Warren Niebuhr

Latino Literature: A Guide to Reading Interests
Edited by Sara E. Martínez

Teen Chick Lit: A Guide to Reading Interests
Christine Meloni

Now Read This III: A Guide to Mainstream Fiction
Nancy Pearl and Sarah Statz Cords

Gay, Lesbian, Bisexual, Transgender and Questioning Teen Literature

A Guide to Reading Interests

Carlisle K. Webber

Genreflecting Advisory Series
Diana Tixier Herald, Series Editor

LIBRARIES UNLIMITED

AN IMPRINT OF ABC-CLIO, LLC
Santa Barbara, California • Denver, Colorado • Oxford, England

Library of Congress Cataloging-in-Publication Data

Webber, Carlisle K.
Gay, lesbian, bisexual, transgender, and questioning teen literature : a guide to
  reading interests / Carlisle K. Webber.
      p. cm. — (Genreflecting advisory series)
  Includes bibliographical references and indexes.
  ISBN 978-1-59158-506-0 (acid-free paper) 1. Young adult literature,
American—Bibliography. 2. Young adult fiction, American—Stories, plots, etc.
3. Sexual minority youth—Juvenile literature—Bibliography. 4. Libraries—Special
collections—Sexual minorities. 5. Libraries—Special collections—Young adult literature.
6. Teenagers—Books and reading—United States. I. Title.
Z1232.W43 2010
[PS374.Y57]
808.8'0353—dc22   2010002577

14 13 12 11 10   1 2 3 4 5

This book is also available on the World Wide Web as an eBook.
Visit www.abc-clio.com for details.

Libraries Unlimited
An Imprint of ABC-CLIO, LLC

ABC-CLIO, LLC
130 Cremona Drive, P.O. Box 1911
Santa Barbara, California 93116-1911

This book is printed on acid-free paper ∞
Manufactured in the United States of America

For Elsie McAvoy, because we never forget our first great teacher (especially those who encourage us to read)

Contents

Acknowledgments

Thanks first and foremost to Di Herald, who encouraged me to write this book; to Bonnie Kunzel, who introduced us; and to editrix Barbara Ittner, who told me I was not the worst writer in the world. All research thanks great and small go to Robin Brenner, Ron Coleman, Kristin Fletcher-Spear, Kat Kan, Jack Martin, Tina Steed, Snow Wildsmith, and Eva Volin. This book would not have been possible without reassurance and support from Ilene Lefkowitz, Molly Johnson, and the Flavorettes: Baby Mama, Smartie, and Gigglz . . . better known as Sophie Brookover, Liz Burns, and Melissa Rabey.

Introduction

Why You're Reading This Book

You want to learn more about what books are available by, for, and about gay, lesbian, bisexual, transgender, queer, and questioning teens. If that's the case, you are in the right place. This book is intended as a guide to GLBTQ literature for teens—a guide that will help librarians build or develop their collections and find read-alikes and books that teens who read GLBTQ literature will enjoy. This guide is not meant as a primer on library or educational services to GLBTQ teens. Nor is it a history of GLBTQ teen literature. It is a guide to assist you in putting teen readers together with the GLBTQ books that meet their reading interests. It is also meant to help you see the wide variety of books available for your collections and to assist you in making the most informed decisions possible about the acquisition of books and other resources that interest GLBTQ teens and their friends. You might not have any of these books in your collection, or you might already have a popular collection of GLBTQ novels with a devoted readership. In either case, this book can serve as a way to check your collection to see its strengths and weaknesses for serving your GLBTQ population. Because it groups titles into specific interest areas, it can also help you find read-alikes or compose thematic lists for your Web site, newsletter, or to print and hand out.

Why Are Teen Books with GLBTQ Content Important?

"Gay teens coming out earlier to peers and family," trumpeted *USA Today* on February 7, 2007.[1] According to the article, 3,200 gay–straight alliances were registered at high schools across the nation. A 2006 Gallup Poll[2] revealed that 52 percent of Generation Y believes that homosexuality is "acceptable." Gen Y is used to seeing gay and lesbian characters on TV shows, from *ER*'s Dr. Kerry Weaver to *Buffy the Vampire Slayer*'s Willow Rosenberg. The class of teens graduating from high school in 2012 does not remember television sitcoms without openly gay characters; they were three years old when "The Puppy Episode, Part 1" of the show *Ellen*, in which protagonist Ellen comes out, first aired. On television and in newspapers they see debates over whether gay and lesbian couples should be granted the right to marry or have the rights to bear and adopt children.

Meanwhile, teens see cars all around them adorned with rainbow flag and pink triangle bumper stickers, and although they may not know the historical significance of these symbols, they do know that they stand for gay pride. In the last ten years, the number of quality books for and about GLBTQ teens has increased, and these books are regularly named to YALSA lists such as Best Books for Young Adults and Popular Paperbacks for Young Adults. Today's teens, even if they are not gay or do not know anyone who is, are familiar with the concept of and debates over homosexuality and gender identity. The library is a place where all teens should expect equal treatment and equal representation of their ideas and personalities.

Librarians who want to serve a diverse population and have many viewpoints in their collections are also limited in one major way beyond space and money: They cannot put on the shelves what no one has yet written or published. Even when the stories are written and published, librarians are limited in collection development because of policies requiring that a book be reviewed by a professional journal before it can go into a library's collection. Books by small and/or independent presses, some of which focus on diverse or gay and lesbian literature, do not get the same space in review journals as books published by larger houses. When it comes to GLTBQ books, quantity isn't enough, even if you're desperate to fill holes in a collection. You're better off having fewer, high-quality books that aren't as diverse as you'd like them to be. Time will give us the diverse, high-quality books we hunger for. By all means, familiarize yourself with small press titles, but before adding them to the collection, make sure they meet the same standards of editing and writing quality as other books in the subject area.

Who Reads GLBTQ Literature

The main readership of the books described in this book is GLBTQ teens. In addition, however, readers with GLBTQ friends or family, or who wonder if they are gay (this is where the Q comes in), or even those who are curious about gay people and the gay culture, are drawn to these books.

Keep in mind that in some of the books annotated here, GLBTQ issues do not necessarily take center stage—they are simply presented as a fact of life. This generally reflects teen experiences today. In the GLBTQ subgenre, however, you will want to conduct a thorough readers' advisory interview before making recommendations, because the content and mood of a book and the main character's feelings about his or her sexuality are key elements in matching the right book to the reader.

Just because a character is not gay or lesbian on the page does not mean that he or she isn't gay/lesbian offstage. Consider J. K. Rowling's speech in New York in October 2007, in which she revealed that Harry Potter's mentor, Albus Dumbledore, was gay: In a first-person or limited third-person book like those in the Harry Potter series, the reader does not fully experience any viewpoint but the main character's. If that character is not concerned with the sexuality of other people in his or her life, it's not going to factor into the book. After the book's publication, the author may reveal that there were GLBTQ characters in the book that never got screen time, or may not reveal anything at all. Had the Harry Potter series used an omniscient perspective, it is entirely possible that readers may have learned about Dumbledore's sexuality on page 1 of *Harry Potter and the Sorcerer's Stone*, or it may never have been important enough to the story line to be revealed at all.

Scope and Organization

This guide covers books in English, both fiction and nonfiction, with GLBTQ themes and content, most published in the last decade but including a few classic, older titles. The titles are grouped into chapters that reflect reader interest and publishing trends and are subdivided into more focused lists. Books are listed alphabetically by author and then title; books in series are listed in publication order below the series name. For series that have no definite titles, a working title has been used for convenience and is enclosed in brackets, for example, [Cyd Charisse].

Unlike adult GLBTQ literature, there has not yet been much genre fiction published for teen GLBTQ readers. Instead, broad themes, such as "coming out" and "first love," predominate. Thus, a single chapter covers several genres, whereas an entire chapter is devoted to the theme "coming-of-age" The detailed table of contents will guide you through the structure of the book.

Terms and Acronyms Used

- **GLBTQ** stands for gay, lesbian, bisexual, transgender, and questioning (or sometimes queer). In some places, you may see this collective adjective as LGBTI: lesbian, gay, bisexual, transgender, and intersex. Both are acceptable for library collection development purposes. There are many words and phrases associated with GLBTQ literature and the GLBTQ community, which you may encounter while doing research into your GLBTQ collection. The individual letters of this acronym are used at the end of each annotation to indicate which term applies to that book. While reading this book, you can take the terms to mean the following:

    Gay: A person who identifies as male and is sexually attracted to other males. Books with gay characters include *Rainbow Boys* by Alex Sanchez and *Twelve Long Months* by Brian Malloy.

    Lesbian: A person who identifies as female and is sexually attracted to other females. Books with lesbian characters include *Down to the Bone* by Mayra Lazara Dole and *Annie on My Mind* by Nancy Garden.

    Bisexual: A person who identifies as either male or female and is sexually attracted to both males and females.

    Transgender: Biologically, a person who was born with the physical characteristics of a male or female, but identifies as a member of the opposite sex. Transgender (or transsexual) people do not feel comfortable in the physical gender they were born with. When speaking about a transgender person or character, it is proper to describe him or her as the gender with which he or she identifies. In other words, a male-to-female transgender is correctly addressed and described as "she." Transgender people can be straight, gay/lesbian, or bisexual. Some transgender persons eventually undergo gender reassignment surgery, in which they biologically become their preferred gender. The Human Rights Campaign reports that anywhere from 0.25 to 1 percent of the U.S. population is transgender (www.hrc.org/issues/transgender/9598.htm). Books that address transgender people include *Luna* by Julie Anne Peters and *Parrotfish* by Ellen Wittlinger.

Intersexual/Intersex: In one of about every 2,000 births, a baby is born with both male and female sex characteristics; these people are labeled "intersex." Intersex people may identify as male, female, neither, or both. They may be straight, gay/lesbian, or bisexual.

Questioning: Although "questioning" in young adult literature usually describes a character who is questioning whether he or she is gay or lesbian, as the market for GLBTQ teen literature expands in years to come, it may describe teens who are questioning not only their sexuality and sexual preferences, but their gender identity as well.

Queer: This term has long been used as a slur against GLBTQ people, but very recently the GLBTQ community has begun to reclaim it, using it as a catchall term for those who do not unquestioningly identify as straight or with one specific gender. One memorable example of a queer character in YA literature is Billy Bloom in *Freak Show* by James St. James.

Slash: "Slash" is a term that goes back to fans of the original *Star Trek* television series. Fans of the show would sometimes write their own stories (called "fanfiction") about what could have happened before, during (offstage), or after the run of the series. Stories in which Captain Kirk and Mr. Spock maintained a professional relationship or platonic friendship were designated as "Kirk&Spock" in their header (somewhat like their bibliographic) information. If Kirk and Spock were involved romantically or sexually, the story was designated in its header information as Kirk/Spock; using the slash instead of the ampersand told the reader what kind of story to expect. Eventually, the term "slash" evolved to describe not just stories about Kirk and Spock, but also those about all male–male romantic pairings in fanfiction. Male–female pairings are referred to as "het," for "heterosexual."

The term does not apply to works created outside the fan world. David Levithan's *Boy Meets Boy* should not be termed "slash" because it is an original work with characters created by the author. On the other hand, a fan-created story in which Harry Potter and Ron Weasley enter into a romantic relationship is definitely worthy of the term "slash."

"Slash" appears in this list of definitions because often when GLBTQ books are discussed on professional YA literature listservs, inevitably someone mentions slash fan fiction as a reading option for GLBTQ teens. This is not illegal or immoral, nor will it hurt any readers, but it is not the best path a librarian doing readers' advisory for GLBTQ teens can take. Currently there is no law barring the creation of slash fanfiction, although there is a constant question among fan writers about what constitutes copyright infringement and fair use. Some authors prefer that fans not write fanfiction about their books at all, but that is true of all types of stories, not just slash. Slash may be written in standard prose or it be made into *doujinshi*, fan-created comics. It is interesting to note that most slash fanfiction is written and read by women (straight, bisexual, and lesbian). Because these stories are fan created and not produced for money, you cannot print them and add them to your collection, and due to the open nature of fandom on the Internet, it is not recommended that you point a first-time reader of GLBTQ works to slash fanfiction, because much of it is poorly written and lacks editing. Fanfiction also requires knowledge of canon characters and relationships prior to being read, and your patrons may or may not have that knowledge.

Although slash concerns male–male relationships, most of it is written by and for women and girls.

Femslash (also femmeslash): Slash fanfiction with female–female pairings instead of male–male. *Empress of the World* by Sara Ryan, an original work about lesbians, is not femmeslash, but a story in which Veronica Mars and Lilly Kane from the television show *Veronica Mars* are romantically involved is. Although femslash is not as popular as male–male slash, it does have a solid, dedicated readership.

- **Shonen-ai (also shounen-ai):** Shonen-ai is an older term for manga, or Japanese comics, which focused on a romantic and sometimes sexual relationship between two young men. Usually the young men are drawn as very beautiful, even androgynous. The term shonen-ai has fallen out of favor, replaced with the term "boys love." The decline in the use of the term is tied to its association with adult–adolescent relationships, which are not the focus of boys love manga. Relationships in shonen-ai manga could be romantic, angsty, or just poetic.

  Boys love (sometimes boyslove or boys' love or boy's love, abbreviated BL): This is the new, more acceptable term for manga and anime that focuses on young male romantic relationships. Unlike its shonen-ai predecessors, BL manga is more likely to have a happy or romantic ending. Boys love, unlike the term "slash," can refer to original works as well as fan-created works.

  Yaoi: Pronounced "YOW-ee," this term also refers to manga about male–male relationships, and the art is often similar to BL manga, but unlike BL, yaoi stories are sexually explicit and aimed at an older audience. Like slash, they are mostly created and read by women.

  Shoujo-ai: This term refers to manga focusing on romantic relationships between two women and is no longer widely used.

  Yuri: A more modern, popular, and inclusive name for shoujo-ai, from the Japanese word meaning "lily." Yuri can refer to original as well as fan-created works.

Awards and Honors

Award-winning books are identified using the following symbol 🌳, and the awards and honors are listed following the annotation, using the acronyms listed below. These awards are particularly pertinent to GLBTQ literature for teens:

- **BBYA:** Best Books for Young Adults is a yearly list created by YALSA that highlights the outstanding books published in a year. BBYA takes into consideration a book's quality as well as its popularity; every year teens are invited to share their opinions about books with the BBYA committee. The BBYA list archive is available at http://ala.org/ala/yalsa/booklistsawards/bestbooksya/bestbooksyoung.cfm.

- **PPYA**: Popular Paperbacks for Young Adults is dedicated to producing themed and genre lists of teen books on various topics, including sports, horror, science fiction, and nonfiction. For these YALSA lists, trends and popularity with teens are more important than quality. The PPYA list archive is available at http://ala.org/ala/yalsa/booklistsawards/popularpaperback/popularpaper backs.cfm.

- **GGNT:** Great Graphic Novels for Teens recommends graphic novels written for a young adult audience that have "proven or potential appeal to the personal reading tastes of teens."

- **QP:** Quick Picks for Reluctant Young Adult Readers "suggests items for recreational reading that have wide appeal to teens who, for whatever reason, do not like to read." Books that appear on QP may be fiction or nonfiction and in any format; photo essays and graphic novels are just two that often show up on this list.

Grade Levels

The suggested reading levels for the entries are shown using VOYA's (Voice of Youth Advocates, http://voya.com) age designations and appear at the end of the bibliographic information:

> **M** middle school (grades 6–8)
>
> **J** junior high (grades 7–9)
>
> **S** senior high (grades 9–12)
>
> **A/YA** adult/young adult (adult books of interest to young adult readers)

These terms are also included in the subject index at the end of this guide. The guide also includes an author/title index and a keyword index, providing multiple points of access for each book. the books have been placed according to the main theme or genre of the book. Because some books in this guide can fit into two or more categories (historical fiction and social issues, for example, or first love and humor), keywords indicating these other categories have been included below these entries only. The keywords identify titles that can fill two or more readers' advisory needs.

Ultimately, it is hoped that this guide will help you develop a greater awareness of GLBTQ literature for teens and better serve those who enjoy reading it.

Notes

1. Marilyn Elias, "Gay Teens Coming Out Earlier to Peers and Family," *USA Today*, February 11, 2007.

2. http://www.gallup.com/poll/21829/american-teenagers-split-gay-marriage.aspx

Chapter 1

Coming-of-Age

Who am I?

Where do I fit in?

What's in my future?

Every teenager has these questions. If they didn't, YA literature would be boring, if it existed at all. Every teen is curious about sex to some degree. For those who don't believe they fit heterosexual or gender norms, their sexuality can be the cause of much wondering and heartache. Does being gay or lesbian automatically cause sadness and depression? Absolutely not. Many of the books in this section show that same-sex relationships have all the dimension of opposite-sex relationships, complete with love, happiness, confusion, and ultimately, self-discovery. What a gay or lesbian character has to contend with that his or her straight counterpart doesn't is the question of how, if at all, to come out to friends and loved ones. For many, stating aloud that "I'm gay" could lead to changes in their lives they hadn't anticipated.

Some GLBTQ teens find coming out liberating, and doing so makes their current relationships, romantic or otherwise, stronger. To come out to others, they must first come out to themselves, an act that requires self-confidence and confidence in the reactions of the people around them. Coming out can be isolating and frightening, too. A teen who comes out takes the risk of losing his or her entire support network of friends and family. Many different kinds of reactions to a character's coming out are possible, and many are shown in the books in this chapter.

Where other books in this guide offer stories in which a character's sexuality is just one point in the overall scheme of the book, the books in this chapter bring sexual identity front and center. In this chapter are books on GLBTQ identity (answering the question "Am I gay?), coming out ("Should I tell others I'm gay? If so, how?"), and first love. One important thing to note is that although the books here are divided along those lines, many fit into two or more categories. A book about GLBTQ identity may revolve around the story of the character's first romance, for example. The categories here serve as a guide to the primary emphasis of each book.

GLBTQ Identity (IMRU?)

"I'm nobody! Who are you? Are you nobody, too?" Though Emily Dickinson probably wasn't referring to adolescent identity when she wrote those lines, they do represent the way many teenagers feel. They are at a point in their lives where they are establishing independence but still need guidance. They feel alone, as if no one understands what they're going through or how they feel. Often they're not sure what they want, but feel the pressure to make long-term decisions about their lives. Add to this the questioning of one's sexuality, and you've got a teen who needs to know more than anything that he or she is not alone in the world.

Identity isn't always about sex or sexuality. The books in this section do focus on identity, but every character in these books is more than just his or her sexuality. These protagonists are interested in everything from art to politics, which is why they are popular with a variety of readers.

Knowing that there is someone else in the world who not only understands them, but loves them, is important to GLBTQ teens. Finding others like them means that they can be confident in their own identities.

Brett, Catherine.

S.P. Likes A.D. The Women's Press, 1989. **J**

S.P. is Stephanie Powell, who is trying to sort out her more-than-platonic feelings for A.D., Anne Delaney. Stephanie's biggest question, however, isn't whether or not Anne likes her as well, but whether she really identifies as a lesbian or if her feelings for Anne are a passing crush, a minor infatuation. Stephanie meets an older lesbian couple through her work on a dinosaur sculpture, and her art teacher is gay. Her father expresses homophobic sentiments, but her best friend isn't too bothered by the idea that Stephanie thinks she may be a lesbian. (L)

Brothers, Meagan.

Debbie Harry Sings in French. Holt, 2008. **J** **S**

Questions about the definitions of sexuality and gender are raised here. Goth Johnny lands in the hospital after his alcoholism, his way of dealing with having to be the man of the house, nearly kills him. In rehab, Johnny becomes fascinated by the music of Blondie. He dons women's clothing, not because he is confused about his gender, but because he wants to emulate Blondie's lead singer, Debbie Harry, whose strength and attitude inspire him. Upon his release he moves from Florida to South Carolina, where he meets Maria. Their shared love of punk music and subsequent friendship help Johnny on his way to recovery. (Q)

Brown, Rita Mae.

Rubyfruit Jungle. Bantam, 1980. **A/YA**

Although originally published for an adult audience, *Rubyfruit Jungle* has become a classic story of the lesbian experience. Molly Bolt has been compared to Huck Finn. Born out of wedlock, Molly is taken in by a poor couple who want her to lead a productive life. She is not a typical girl, but is rather outgoing and bold with boys and is a lesbian. Not everyone in her community is tolerant of her sexuality, but as

Molly heads to college and then to New York, her resolve and wit carry her through difficult times. (L)

Keywords: classic

De Oliveira, Eddie.

🏵 *Lucky*. Scholastic, 2004. **J** **S**

After his first year at university, Sam Smith reflects on his past and wonders exactly what his sexual identity is. Soccer, or as British Sam calls it, football, brings him together with Toby, who introduces him to gay nightlife and encourages Sam to be more honest with himself about his sexuality. With much British slang and humor reminiscent of Louise Rennison's novels, Sam confesses to both himself and the reader that he might indeed be the type to fancy boys, and he looks to his friends for acceptance and guidance. (G, B, Q)

Awards/honors: PPYA

Keywords: humor

Donovan, John.

I'll Get There. It Better Be Worth the Trip. Harper & Row, 1969. **J** **S**

After his parents' divorce, Davy is raised by his grandmother outside Boston. When she dies, Davy is forced to move to New York to live with his alcoholic mother. Davy's best friend is his dog Fred, until he meets Douglas Altschuler in his geography class. While playing with Fred one afternoon, Davy and Douglas share a kiss. This leads to confusion and some anger on Davy's part, amplified by the attitude toward homosexuality in the late 1960s. This is the first book published for teens with a main character dealing with homosexual thoughts and actions and remains an important work in the genre today. (G)

Keywords: 1960s; classic; historical setting

Eugenides, Jeffrey.

🏵 *Middlesex*. Picador, 2003. **A/YA**

Calliope Stephanides, born in 1960, identified wholly as a girl until 1974, when she discovers that she is genetically if not outwardly physically male. Calliope, aka Cal, narrates the story of his grandparents' relationship, then his parents'. The reader learns that Cal's grandparents are brother and sister and his parents are related as well, and because of this Cal has inherited a gene that caused him to be born with both male and female sex organs. The story spans the globe, exploring ideas of gender and family. (Q)

Awards/honors: Pulitzer Prize

Keywords: historical setting

Ferris, Jean.

Eight Seconds. Harcourt, 2000. **J** **S**

John lives with his loving family in rodeo country, a stereotypically masculine environment. During the summer, his father sends him to rodeo school for five days, where he develops a love of bull-riding and meets confident, low-key Kit. After returning home for the summer, John and Kit meet a few more times. John learns that Kit is gay, and although this causes many bullying problems for both John and Kit, Kit's honesty sets John on a path to being honest with himself, questioning and discovering his own sexuality. (G)

Hartinger, Brent.

🏵 *Geography Club*. HarperTempest, 2003. **J** **S**

Russel Middlebrook is the only gay teen at his high school, or so he's convinced. After finding out that his best friend is bisexual and one of the popular jocks is gay, the four of them get together with three other students to form a gay–straight alliance, which they call the Geography Club to avoid censure by the school administration. Russel experiences his first love and his first heartbreak and has to quickly face the public when word gets out that he's gay. Humor and realistic dialogue are the book's strengths. (G, B)

Awards/honors: PPYA; Lambda Literary Award finalist

Kerr, M. E.

"Hello," I Lied. HarperCollins, 1997. **S**

When Lang Penner's mother gets a job working for retired, reclusive rock star Ben Nevada, she moves them to Nevada's Hamptons estate. Lang is encouraged to come out by Ben's lover, a move that Lang's mother, who does not fully accept his sexuality, doesn't much like. Also at the estate is Huguette, Nevada's illegitimate daughter from France. Lang finds Huguette charming and falls in love with her, which makes him question his sexuality, especially after they have sex. At the end of the book, however, Lang still identifies as gay, noting that sexuality is not always a definite, fixed thing. (G)

Larson, Rodger.

What I Know Now. Holt, 1997. **M** **J**

Set in 1957, this novel is more about the desire to belong and be confident in one's identity than it is about coming out. When Dave's parents split up, his mother takes him to her childhood home, the "Home Place." There, Dave meets Gene Tole, a landscaper who is everything his father isn't: sensitive, gentle, and thoughtful. Dave doesn't realize Gene is gay at first, but he does eventually fall in love with him. Dave's slowly unfolding realizations lead him to see that there are many ways men can act and interact. (G)

Keywords: historical setting

Mac, Carrie.

Crush. Orca, 2006. **S**

After Hope's parents leave her with her sister Joy in New York City and go to Thailand to build schools, Hope takes a job as a nanny for a lesbian couple. At first Hope is not sure how she feels about working for them and living in their spare room, but she is homesick and in need of companionship other than Joy, so she takes the position. She also falls for Nat, a nineteen-year-old florist biker chick. Hope's feelings for Nat confuse her, but her employers help her work through her questions about her sexuality. (L)

Medina, Nico.

🌑 *The Straight Road to Kylie*. Simon Pulse, 2007. **S**

Life couldn't get much better for Jonathan Parrish, who is out and confident in his sexuality. He loves being "one of the girls" and hanging out and partying with his best friend Joanna. His biggest celebrity crush is not Orlando Bloom or Brad Pitt, but Kylie Minogue. Then, at a party, Jonathan gets wasted and loses his virginity . . . to a girl. Now that he's known for being able to please a girl sexually, the rich and manipulative Laura Schulberg wants to have him for her boyfriend. But are the Kylie Minogue tickets that Laura can get for Jonathan worth compromising who he knows he is? (G)

Awards/honors: PPYA

Keywords: humor

Nelson, Blake.

Gender Blender. Delacorte, 2006. **M**

In a *Freaky Friday*-esque body switch, Tom and Emma end up living in each other's bodies after they encounter a cursed arrowhead and a trampoline collision. Neither character is truly transgender, intersex, or otherwise uncomfortable in his or her given body, but their experiences living in the body of a member of the opposite sex bring both Tom and Emma, who were not happy about being paired up for a health class project, to a higher understanding of gender roles and body issues. Realistic language reflects the way sixth-graders truly think and talk. (Q)

Peters, Julie Anne.

🌑 *Luna*. Little, Brown, 2004. **J** **S**

Themes of secrecy and self-expression drive this novel. Every night Liam enters his sister Regan's room so he can try on his true identity, that of a girl named Luna. The time has come, Liam has decided, to start presenting himself as Luna to the wider world, dressing in women's clothing and wigs and going out in public. Liam and Regan's friends and family, unfortunately, are not always accepting of who Liam really is. Using realistic situations and dialogue, Peters educates readers on issues and terminology important to transgender persons. (T)

Awards/honors: PPYA; BBYA; National Book Award finalist

Polito, Frank Anthony.

Band Fags! Kensington, 2009. ⬛

Hanging around girls in a just-as-friends way was fine for Jack in elementary school, but now that it's 1982 and he's in high school, the pressure is on to have a girlfriend. Hanging out with girls but not dating them gets Jack, a star trumpet player, and his friend Brad labeled "Band Fags." Brad and Jack are inseparable friends even though they have little in common. Brad knows he's gay, but Jack isn't so sure of his own sexuality. All he knows is that he wants the kind of love that they sing about on the radio. (G)

Keywords: 1980s; historical setting

Drama Queers! Kensington, 2009. ⬛

When he grows up, high school senior Bradley is going to be a famous actor, or so he said on his English paper.

Ryan, P. E.

In Mike We Trust. HarperTeen, 2009. ⬛

Being gay doesn't bother fifteen-year-old Garth, not the way that his short stature does. He's out to his mother, but he asks that she keep his sexuality a secret. Not long after Garth's father dies, his uncle shows up and wants Garth to help collect money for phony charities. When Garth figures out the scam, he has to undo the lies he told to his mother. The theme of trust plays out both between Garth and his mother and between Garth and Adam, who is openly gay and friends with Garth's best friend, Lisa. (G)

Ryan, Sara.

🏵 *Empress of the World.* Viking, 2001. 🅹 ⬛

This summer-camp romance follows aspiring archaeologist Nicola (Nic) to a summer program for gifted high school students, where she immediately falls for Battle Hall Davies. Despite her feelings for Battle and their ensuing roller-coaster relationship, the introspective, analytical Nic also develops a crush on a boy. She keeps her options open because she wants to avoid labeling herself; how can she be a lesbian if she likes boys? Over the summer, she is affected and changed by her new, quirky, artistic friends. Her carefully detailed "field notes" describe new, close friendships and her journey toward self-acceptance sans sexuality labels. (L, B, Q)

Awards/honors: BBYA

Sanchez, Alex.

The God Box. Simon & Schuster, 2008. 🅹 ⬛

Inspired by fan mail he received after the publication of *Rainbow Boys* (annotated in chapter X), in this book Sanchez writes about a young man trying to reconcile his spirituality and his sexuality. Paul lives in a small town in Texas and is very religious. Manuel, the new boy, is the first openly gay person Paul has ever known. Manuel's confidence in his sexuality alienates many of the boys at their high school, but Paul is interested in Manuel's friendship. Manuel tells Paul that he is gay *and* Christian, and this makes Paul question his own sexuality as well as his faith. (G)

Selvadurai, Shyam.

Swimming in the Monsoon Sea. **Tundra Books, 2005.** **S** **A/YA**

Amrith, age fourteen, is living with his adoptive family in Colombo, Sri Lanka, circa 1980, when his cousin Niresh visits from Canada. Amrith discovers many secrets about his family when Niresh brings Amrith's father to his home. As Amrith gets to know Niresh better, he realizes that his feelings for Niresh go beyond friendship and family. During Niresh's visit, Amrith acts in a school production of *Othello*, and at times his anger and behavior mirror that character's. (G)

Keywords: historical setting

Sloan, Brian.

A Really Nice Prom Mess. **Simon & Schuster, 2005.** **S**

It's an unforgettable night of disaster when senior Cameron tries to hide from his prom date, Virginia, the fact that he's gay and would much rather be at the prom with his football-player boyfriend. Virginia sees right through Cameron and decides to drown her sorrows in alcohol, and Cameron has to flee from his prom mess after he gets caught kissing Shane's date. What follows is a Daniel Pinkwater-esque comedy of errors that introduces more strange characters at every turn. In one night, Cameron learns a lot about himself, and he wakes up the next morning a slightly changed man. (G, L)

Keywords: humor

Soehnlein, K. M.

The World of Normal Boys. **Kensington, 2000.** **A/YA**

"Normal" boys like his father, younger brother, and uncle, who are crude and make a habit of insulting other people, elude Robin. As he begins his freshman year in high school in the late 1970s, Robin, who enjoys Broadway music and helping his mother make fashion decisions, tries to be more normal and cool, but his little brother's accident puts a strain on his entire family. Robin also begins a relationship with Todd, his older next-door neighbor, who will kiss him one minute and make homophobic remarks the next. In his alienation, Robin engages in many standard teen risks: drugs, cutting school, and so on. (G)

Keywords: 1970s; historical setting

St. James, James.

Freak Show. **Dutton, 2007.** **J** **S**

Flamboyant drag queen Billy is transplanted from Connecticut to conservative Florida. His joyous, mile-a-minute dialogue, filled with pop culture references, complements his passion for Vivienne Westwood clothing.

Unfortunately, not everyone at his new school is accepting of Billy's differences. When his classmates physically beat him down, Billy knows he has to come back with flair, so he decides to run for Homecoming Queen. His rise to popularity as an individual among a homogenous group of classmates is reminiscent of Jerry Spinelli's *Stargirl* (Knopf, 2000). Billy describes his sexuality and gender identification as ambiguous, although he does enter into a romance with another boy. (G, Q)

Keywords: humor

Taylor, William.

The Blue Lawn. **Alyson Publications, 1999.** **J** **S**

Opposites attract in this New Zealand story of fifteen-year-olds Theo and David. David is quiet and straitlaced, but of the two he is more comfortable in his sexuality. Drawn together by a locker room fight, they slowly become a part of each other's lives. Changing seasons parallel the changes in their relationship, which comes to the reader through realistic dialogue. Theo's grandmother, Holocaust survivor Gretel, separates them, believing that she will save them from hurting one another. When the nature of their relationship is revealed, their families and schoolmates are remarkably tolerant. (G)

Velasquez, Gloria.

🎗 *Tommy Stands Alone.* **Arte Publico Press, 1995.** **S**

Tommy's sexuality causes him constant inner torture. His friends often make homophobic remarks, and Tommy, who is gay, keeps his feelings inside. After his friends find a note written to him by another gay boy, David, Tommy tries to commit suicide using alcohol and pills. When the attempt fails, Tommy's best friend Maya asks a counselor, Ms. Martinez, to visit him in the hospital. It is Maya who gives Tommy shelter when his father kicks him out of the family home, and Tommy is forced to confront his feelings in a healthy way. (G)

Awards/honors: BBYA

Walker, Kate.

Peter. **Houghton Mifflin, 1993.** **J** **S**

In order to be a part of a group, fifteen-year-old Peter must hide his love of photography and any emotion that is less than macho. To be accepted by his friends, Peter is supposed to defy rules, both his own and his mother's, and have sex with a girl he doesn't love. In the midst of his personal conflict he meets his brother's friend David, who is gay, and finds himself attracted to David. David is unlike most of Peter's friends, and he encourages Peter to explore his feelings, even if they go against his friends' chauvinistic views. (G)

Winterson, Jeanette.

🎗 *Oranges Are Not the Only Fruit.* **Pandora Press, 1985.** **S**

With offbeat humor, the adopted, unnamed narrator relates her story of being raised a lesbian in an evangelical Christian household. Her mother's choice of bedtime reading is the book of Deuteronomy rather than *Goodnight, Moon*, and by the age of ten she occupies herself by making samplers with eschatological sayings. Not long after her first questioning of the church and its ideas, at fifteen she falls in love with Melanie, a former church member. The author handles the disparities between how the narrator feels and what she's been taught in the church with aplomb, with the narrator eventually leaving the church to live her own life. (L)

Awards/honors: Whitbread Prize winner

Wittlinger, Ellen.

Parrotfish. **Simon & Schuster, 2007.** **S**

Angela knows that even though she has a girl's body, she's really a boy. Over Christmas, she cuts her hair, binds her breasts, and takes the name Grady, actions she has considered for years. Grady's coming out doesn't go well. His father is relatively accepting, but his mother, sister, and best friend are not, and the kids at school certainly don't understand. Grady stays true to who he is and begins to find allies, from a gym teacher to a science nerd, Sebastian. Gender roles and identity are explored in a generally upbeat style. (T)

Wright, Bil.

Sunday You Learn How to Box. **Touchstone, 2000.** **S**

In 1968, in Connecticut's Stratfield Projects, the greatest crime a boy can commit is not robbery or murder, but preferring cerebral activities to physical ones. Thoughtful Louis takes regular beatings on the streets, prompting his mother to set up Sunday matches between Louis and his macho stepfather Ben in the hope that Louis will gain some street survival skills. Louis realizes he's gay as he falls for Ray Anthony Robinson, who is believed to be a hoodlum by the neighbors but assumes a role as Louis's guardian. (G)

Keywords: 1960s; historical setting

Coming Out

A question was posed to the glbtqYAwriters listserv in August 2009: *Are we past the coming-out story?* Author Lee Wind began the discussion as follows, quoting children's book editor Arthur A. Levine:

> Nobody ever complains about a book being another first love story, so why shouldn't there be more coming out stories? And . . . there are precious few minority coming out stories. Also, Bisexual and Transgender [sic] stories are scarce.

The question "Do we need another book about coming out?" is one librarians should keep in mind when developing a collection. What Wind notes is true: Stories of bisexual and transgender characters are far outnumbered by stories about their gay and lesbian peers. Minority characters are also underrepresented in GLBTQ and coming-out stories. In a library where there might only be space and budget for the few GLBTQ books that circulate, the question of adding what seems like "just another coming-out story" in favor of stories that have GLBTQ characters but take more risks in genre, literary quality, and format is a very real one. There is no one right answer to the question of what to add to which collection, because each community readership has different needs and wants.

Teens value the opinions of their friends and family, and they are highly sensitive to peer pressure. This combination of traits can make life very difficult for teens who are considering coming out. They can never be sure how their peers and families will react, because even open-minded people who believe in treating others fairly will sometimes react differently to knowing someone gay in real life. That uncertainty is often stifling for GLBTQ teens, who not only face the questions, "Who am I, and what do I want to do with my life?" but also ask, "Will I have any support as I move into adulthood?" Not knowing what others will think keeps many GLBTQ teens in the closet. On the other hand, coming out can be a freeing or affirming experience, and in these books often there is peer pressure from other gay teens for a character to come out to family or school friends.

The characters in the books in this section share one trait: They have all chosen to come out to their friends, their families, or both. Some receive love and understanding from those close to them; others are not so lucky. These books capture the fact that even loving families and friends might not know how to offer support to someone who comes out to them.

Bantle, Lee.

David Inside Out. Holt, 2009. **S**

Running is David's outlet for stress, until he develops a crush on a fellow member of the track team. David is out to himself but not to anyone else. He dates girls and maintains the façade of being straight. He's also reluctant to associate with his best friend, Eddie, after Eddie comes out to him. Sean, his crush, is closeted but not above having sex with David. David's relationships with Sean, Eddie, and his (girl) friend Kick help him grow and accept himself, even as he endures bullying from a homophobic classmate. (G)

Keywords: sports

Cart, Michael.

🏵 *My Father's Scar*. Simon & Schuster, 1996. **S**

Andy Logan, a freshman in college, reflects on painful as well as precious memories of his childhood and adolescence. The major players in his life include his domineering father and grandmother; his mother, who sides with his father; and his best friend Evan. Evan, who fascinates Andy, comes out, and the reaction in their town is brutal and emotionally destructive to Andy. Andy is attracted to Evan but dares not come out because he fears the same retaliation and ostracism suffered by Evan, and he worries about his father's homophobia. (G)

Awards/honors: BBYA

Ford, Michael Thomas.

Suicide Notes. **HarperCollins, 2008.** **S**

Jeff tells his story from a hospital psychiatric ward. At first he is reluctant to speak about why he's there, preferring to observe his fellow patients, until a sexual encounter with another male patient forces him to reveal why he was committed. During his major breakthrough in therapy, Jeff admits that he has not been honest with himself or anyone else about his sexuality. With the support of his sister, and then of his parents, he is able to be honest and start on the road to recovery. (G)

Goobie, Beth.

Hello, Groin. **Orca, 2006.** **S**

Even the best night with her kind boyfriend Cam can't compare to the sexual tension Dylan feels when she's with her best friend Jocelyn (Jocq). After kissing another girl at a school dance and inciting controversy and public discourse about sex over a book display that she creates, Dylan decides to come clean about her sexuality and tells her family that she's a lesbian. Her parents and sister are loving and accepting, as are her now-ex Cam and Jocelyn. Dylan's courage about her sexuality inspires Jocelyn to accept her own sexuality. (L)

Konigsberg, Bill.

Out of the Pocket. **Dutton, 2008.** **S**

From the outside, everything in high school senior Bobby Framingham's life looks great: He's one of the best football players in California and has scholarship offers from all the right schools. On the inside, Bobby is keeping a big secret: He's gay. Once he comes out he cannot escape being in the spotlight, but Bobby sees himself as "just a regular guy" who happens to like other guys, not someone who can be the poster child for gay athletes. In the sports world, where almost no one is openly gay, Bobby wonders where he fits in. (G)

Keywords: sports

LaRochelle, David.

🏵 *Absolutely, Positively Not.* **Scholastic, 2005.** **M** **J**

Sixteen-year-old Steven DeNarski dates girls and has the perfect excuse for why he's attracted to his male teacher; therefore, he is definitely not gay. For all his hilarious, disastrous attempts to be straight, though, Steven knows the truth about himself: He's absolutely, positively gay. When he tells his best friend Rachel about his sexuality, she encourages him to form a gay–straight alliance at school even though he can barely admit his sexuality to himself, much less to the kids at school. Though the author tells the story with humor, Steven's ponderings and need for support are treated with dignity. (G)

Awards/honors: BBYA

Keywords: humor

Murrow, Liza Ketchum.

Twelve Days in August. Holiday House, 1993. **J** **S**

Soccer and his girlfriend Kai are sixteen-year-old Todd's primary interests. Everything about his varsity soccer career is going as planned, until twins Alex and Rita move to town. Alex turns out to be a star soccer player, and this upsets Todd's teammate Randy. Randy, who suspects Alex may be gay, starts spreading rumors about Alex's sexuality and encourages the other members of the soccer team to bully Alex. Todd plays along with Randy until his uncle, a picture of normalcy, reveals that he, too, is gay. (G)

Keywords: sports

Coyote Blue. (Sequel). Simon & Schuster, 1997. **J** **S**

In this follow-up to *Twelve Days in August*, Alex has troubling dreams about his best friend Tito, who still lives in their former home in California. Alex's father, a screenwriter, is asked to work in Hollywood over the summer, and Alex follows him when he cannot contact Tito. After he does some searching, Alex learns that Tito is living in a trailer with his boyfriend and that his father threw him out when Tito came out to him. At first Alex leaves Tito, but when the two reunite, Alex admits that he is gay. (G)

Awards/honors: Lambda Literary Award

Keywords: sports

Peters, Julie Anne.

Keeping You a Secret. Little, Brown, 2004. **J** **S**

All her life, Holland has been a model student. She has a great boyfriend and the promise of an Ivy League future. Then she meets out, proud lesbian Cece and begins to question her romantic feelings for her boyfriend. Holland and Cece's relationship quickly becomes serious and intense. Cece gives Holland the strength to admit that she'd like to pursue a future as an artist, and to come out to her mother. Her mother's reaction is disheartening; she throws Holland out of the house. However, thanks to Cece, Holland is able to start rebuilding her life, though it is quite different from the one she had. (L)

Awards/honors: PPYA

Sanchez, Alex.

So Hard to Say. Simon & Schuster, 2004. **M** **J**

Xiomara, aka Xio, is in eighth grade, outgoing and comfortable with who she is. Frederick, the new boy in her class, has just moved to California from Wisconsin. From the moment Xio lends Frederick her pen, she wants to ask him out. The trouble is, Frederick doesn't really think he likes Xio that way. In fact, he's pretty sure he doesn't like girls that way at all. But how is he going to break that news to Xio? This book is geared for a middle-school audience, told in alternating viewpoints between Xio and Frederick. (G)

Awards/honors: Lambda Literary Award winner

First Love

Love is all around in YA literature. Whether the protagonist is a spy, a vampire, or just an everyday high school student, it's difficult to find a YA book these days that doesn't have an element of romance in it. First love, regardless of sexuality, can be filled with both joy and drama. For some GLBTQ teens, finding their first love occurs simultaneously with their discovery of their own sexuality.

Because these are YA stories, the focus is on finding that first, memorable love rather than the "happily ever after" that comes in adult romances. Teens who can't get enough romance regardless of sexuality might also enjoy the titles in the "Teen Romance" section of chapter 2.

Aciman, Andre.

Call Me by Your Name. **Farrar, Straus & Giroux, 2007.** **A/YA**
Six weeks in Italy bring romance for sensitive, emotional Elio, who spares the reader none of his feelings. His father, a professor, recruits a research assistant from an American university. The assistant, Oliver, and Elio begin a sun-drenched friendship, then a romance that they keep a secret. Oliver returns to the United States, and the two keep in touch via infrequent letters and postcards. Absence makes Elio's heart grow fonder, and over the years he continues to feel passion for Oliver, which is finally consummated years after their first meeting. (G)

Behdun, Tea.

Gravel Queen. **Simon & Schuster, 2003.** **J** **S**
Aspiring filmmaker Aurin, in the summer between her junior and senior years, falls for Neila. What follows is an exploration of first love, and how Aurin's new romance strains her relationships with her friends Kenney and Fred. Aurin finds support from Fred, who has identified as gay for some time, but Kenney is jealous and resentful of Aurin and Neila's relationship. Because of its short length (160 pages) and touches of humor, this may be appealing to reluctant readers. (G, L)

Burd, Nick.

The Vast Fields of Ordinary. **Dial, 2009.** **S**
It's Dade's last summer before college, and he's ready to leave his small Iowa town and his boring job. Though he's out to his friends and family, he hasn't ever seriously dated a boy. Secretly, he's hooking up with Pablo, a jock who not only treats Dade like dirt, but has a girlfriend. Then Dade meets Alex, who is anything but boring and suburban. Alex becomes Dade's escape from his parents' failing marriage, and their relationship gives Dade a wider understanding of other people's emotions. (G, L)

Garden, Nancy.

Annie on My Mind. **Farrar, Straus & Giroux, 1982.** 🇯 🇸

One of the earliest "happy" lesbian love stories for young adults, this work has become a classic. Liza and Annie meet at a museum and become inseparable despite their superficial differences. (Liza wants to be an architect, and Annie is a musician.) Over time they realize that their feelings for each other go beyond friendship. They are temporarily parted, however, when their relationship is discovered by a parent from Liza's school. Although Liza and Annie face harassment from their peers and the separation of college, the story's end will reassure readers that love can indeed conquer social obstacles. (L)

Keywords: classic

Good Moon Rising. **Farrar, Straus & Giroux, 1996.** 🇯 🇸

Jan knows she's star material. Years of acting experience convince her that she'll land the lead in her high school's production of *The Crucible*. She loses the part to newcomer Kerry, but is offered the opportunity to assistant-direct the play. The drama teacher falls ill and must withdraw from directing, leaving Jan to put all of her acting and coaching skills to use as she takes over production of the show. Life begins to imitate art as Jan and Kerry fall for each other, their relationship becomes mostly public, and a homophobic cast member begins his own hysterical lesbian witch hunt. (L)

Guy, Rosa.

Ruby. **Viking, 1976.** 🇸

Ruby, originally from the West Indies, moves to Harlem with her father and sister. She is lonely in her new home because her mother has died, her father works away from home much of the time, and her sister doesn't do much talking. At school, Ruby meets dynamic Daphne and the two begin a friendship, then a romance. Issues surrounding religion, sexuality, and race are covered here, and it is important to note that this is one of the first books published with lesbian content, and also one of a handful that feature African American characters. (L)

Keywords: classic

Hautzig, Deborah.

Hey, Dollface. **Morrow, 1978.** 🇲 🇯

Fifteen-year-old New Yorkers Chloe and Val meet at private school and become friends. As they spend more time together, the girls develop a sexual attraction for each other. Ultimately, they never act on their ideas; they do love each other, but they do not identify as lesbians. Val, the narrator, acknowledges that her feelings about Chloe do not necessarily define her identity. This ambiguity of sexual identity is something still relevant to teens today, even though the book is over thirty years old. (L, Q)

Keywords: classic

Hegamin, Tonya.

M+O 4EVR. Houghton Mifflin, 2008. **J** **S**

In a small Pennsylvania town, Opal and Marianne, both African American, are each other's protection from racism. During their freshman year of high school, they grow apart as Marianne experiments with drugs and cuts class while Opal studies hard and gets good grades. Despite their differences, Opal tells Marianne she loves her in a way that Marianne does not return. Marianne commits suicide soon after in a ravine that is rumored to be haunted by a ghost named Hannah. Hannah and Opal have similar stories, which play out as the book progresses. (L)

Kluger, Steve.

My Most Excellent Year: A Novel of Love, Mary Poppins, and Fenway Park. Dial, 2008. **J** **S**

Friendship and trust are the ties that bind in this upbeat novel. In alternating voices, T.C., Ale (short for Alejandra), and Augie write about the course of their friendship (and T.C.'s crush on Ale). T.C. and Augie have declared themselves brothers, there for each other no matter what. Everyone knows that Augie is gay . . . everyone, that is, except Augie. As the story progresses, Augie finally comes out to himself and begins his first romantic relationship with a boy, much to the delight of T.C., Ale, and his parents, Broadway fans who have known since Augie was little that he was gay. (G)

Collections and Anthologies

Short story collections, though not as popular a format as novels, have an important place in YA literature. In one volume, a team of authors may explore just about any theme they want to. These collections focus on themes of sexual identity, coming out, love, and gender identity.

Bauer, Marion Dane, ed.

Am I Blue? Coming Out from the Silence. HarperCollins, 1994. **J** **S**

This collection of eighteen short stories is a classic in the GLBTQ teen genre, featuring stories from established authors such as Lois Lowry, Bruce Coville, M. E. Kerr, and Gregory Maguire. The stories include gay and lesbian viewpoints from both protagonists questioning their own sexuality and those whose stories are affected by the sexuality of a friend or family member. Despite the age of this volume, the stories are still relevant to today's teens. Each story includes a note from the author on the story's creation, giving it a more personal touch for teen readers. (G, L, Q)

Awards/honors: BBYA

Cart, Michael, ed.

How Beautiful the Ordinary: Twelve Stories of Identity. HarperCollins, 2009. **S**

> Regular readers of GLBTQ YA fiction will recognize most of the names in this collection, which includes works by Julie Anne Peters, Francesca Lia Block, and David Levithan. Diversity in both format and types of sexuality, plus the quality writing, make this a valuable addition to library collections. Two stories in the collection center on transgender characters; one is a short story in verse; and another is in graphic format. Block's story captures the popularity of teens making connections over the Internet and is told entirely in e-mails. (G, L, B, T)

🎗 *Love and Sex: Ten Stories of Truth.* Simon & Schuster, 2001. **S**

> The ten contributing authors to this anthology are all well-known, including Printz honorees Laurie Halse Anderson and Chris Lynch. The stories of particular interest to GLBTQ readers are Emma Donoghue's "The Welcome," in which a British lesbian falls for a male-to-female transgender and wonders what this means about her sexuality, and Michael Lowenthal's sensuous "The Acuteness of Desire," in which a gay boy experiences his first wonderful yet ill-fated romance with another boy. (G, L, T)
>
> **Awards/honors:** BBYA, PPYA

Howe, James, ed.

13: Thirteen Stories That Capture the Agony and Ecstasy of Being Thirteen. Simon & Schuster, 2003. **M**

> As Bruce Coville writes in the opening story of this anthology: "If thirteen is supposed to be an unlucky number, what does it mean that we are forced to go through an entire year with that as our age?" Popular, critically acclaimed young adult authors have contributed to this work, including Meg Cabot, Todd Strasser, and Ann M. Martin. Of particular interest to GLBTQ readers is Alex Sanchez's story, "If You Kiss a Boy," in which Joe kisses his best friend Jamal at the movies and then wonders how it will affect their friendship. (G)

Levithan, David.

How They Met and Other Stories. Knopf, 2008. **S**

> Eighteen short stories are based on one theme: how a couple met. The protagonists are a mix of straight and gay. While Levithan's reputation and popularity give this book broad appeal, readers interested in GLBTQ-specific stories will want to read "Miss Lucy Had a Steamboat," in which a lesbian decides that she will remain alone rather than pursue a girlfriend; "The Princes," which revolves around a bar mitzvah, a boy, and his gay brother; and "Skipping the Prom," in which a boy comes out to his prom date. (G, L)

Peters, Julie Anne.

grl2grl. Little, Brown, 2007. **J** **S**

> This book could also easily fit in chapter 2, "Contemporary Realistic Fiction." Ten stories told in the first person explore female sexuality from the points of view of lesbian and transgender girls. The voices are authentic, often rough. "Boi," about

a female-to-male transgender, makes use of nongender-specific pronouns like "zie," something that may gain popularity in YA literature as more books with transgender characters are published. The stories explore themes of love, sex, homophobia, sex education, and marriage for all people. Peripheral characters, just as in the real world, are neither wholly accepting nor rejecting of lesbians and transgender people. (G, L, T, Q)

Stinson, Kathy.

101 Ways to Dance. **Second Story Press, 2007.** **S**

This slim short story collection (137 pages, plus an author bio and discussion guide) contains stories about straight, gay, and lesbian relationships. Stories of interest to GLBTQ teens include "Between Mars and Venus," in which two girls internally question their feelings for each other; "Waiting for Brian," in which two girls experiment physically; "Micheline and Renee," in which a girl questions what she knows about lesbian relationships after reading a book; and "Ferris Wheel," in which Steve confesses to his friend Tom that he's gay. (G, L)

Summer, Jane, ed.

Not the Only One: Gay and Lesbian Fiction for Teens. **Alyson Publications, 2004.** **J** **S**

This 2004 update of this anthology, originally published in 1994, includes ten new stories from established gay and lesbian authors for both teens and adults, including Brent Hartinger and Michael Thomas Ford. (G, L)

Chapter 2

Contemporary Realistic Fiction

" . . . and also, I'm gay."

For some teens, there is no question about to their sexuality. They know from the start that they are gay/lesbian/bisexual/transgender, and may explain that they have known about their sexuality since they were very young. Their stories may be about their coming out to their friends and/or family, but in the case of these books, it is one of many important life events in a book, rather than a front-and-center exploration of sexuality.

Books like these, in which being gay is an issue but not *the* issue, are a fairly recent phenomenon in YA literature, and an important one. These books recognize that GLBT teens are not "perverse," or "just going through a phase," or "thinking about being gay" and they are not punished for their sexuality via death or disease even though being GLBT may make them the targets of discrimination and/or harassment. These characters face all the same daily issues as their peers—dating and romance, life at school, family, friends, and work—and often their sexuality colors their view of these day-to-day events. In some cases, their attraction to a member of the same sex is what brings them into the plot of the book, and they develop a romance along with their academic or work-related accomplishments. Being gay is an important part of their social context, but in the books that appear in this section, sexuality doesn't necessarily drive the plot.

The range of characters appearing in these novels reflects the diverse makeup of today's teens, promoting the idea that not only are GLBT teens just as normal as everyone else, but stories of their lives should be included along with those of their straight peers. Today's teens live in a society that is more accepting of differences than it was twenty or even ten years ago, but homophobia is still an issue, which schools are sometimes reluctant to openly address. Sensitive, sometimes funny, well-written books dealing with the day-to-day lives of GLBT teens provide role models for today's teens and may give them hope and courage regarding their sexuality, especially in a conflicting world where television shows like *Will and Grace* and *Queer Eye for the Straight Guy* enjoy great popularity in syndication but gays and lesbians are barred from marriage in most states. To date, there are not many books that highlight teens of color who are also GLBTQ. Those that do exist are noted.

One book in particular, James Howe's *The Misfits*, has inspired schools across America to participate in No Name-Calling Week. The No Name-Calling Week Coalition, founded by the Gay, Lesbian, and Straight Education Network (GLSEN) and Simon & Schuster, has forty partner organizations and promotes tolerance to fifth through eighth graders, and the coalition asks that for one week a year, no one call anyone else a derogatory name. This evidences the power of literature, and we can hope that more books will have such positive effects on our society.

The books in this chapter recognize that teens face many coming-of-age events at once, and they promote the idea that though they may not experience exactly what their straight friends do in terms of romance and realization of their sexuality, they are in no way alone.

These books fall into one of four categories. First, "Friends" focuses on books with straight protagonists, with plot points centered around their gay and lesbian friends. Books in the "Family" section are narrated by straight protagonists with gay, lesbian, and transgender family members. The third section shows GLBTQ protagonists in their everyday lives, falling in love. The fourth section contains collections on all three of these themes.

Friends

After love, friendship is probably the most-explored theme in YA fiction. Teens are influenced by their friends and form their friendships around commonalities. Whether they have one good friend or ten, teens value their friendships. Friends provide a point of view that is different from those of parents and guardians. With their friends (and most important, out of view of their parents), teens explore their identities and develop as human beings. GLBTQ teens who might not have a lot of support from their families depend on their friends for love and guidance. This section covers books that feature gay characters as friends, as well as those in which friendship is a theme for a gay protagonist.

Acito, Mark.

How I Paid for College: A Novel of Sex, Theft, Friendship, and Musical Theater. Broadway, 2004. **S**

The laugh-out-loud humor adds dimension to this book, making this a pick for collections whose current GLBTQ collections consist mostly of more serious titles. Edward Zanni looks forward to starting his acting education at Juilliard, until his father marries a gold digger. Now he has to find a way to put himself through school, but he'll never make it on minimum-wage jobs. Edward turns to his girlfriend and the jock he's crushing on to help him with schemes of scholarship fraud and embezzlement. Together they conspire to get Edward into school on a fake scholarship. (G, B)

Keywords: humor

Bargar, Gary.

What Happened to Mr. Forster? **Clarion, 1981.** **M** **J**

Mr. Forster's kindness and tolerance make a big difference in Louis's life in 1950s Kansas. Louis has always been chosen last for teams and called a sissy by his classmates. Mr. Forster helps Louis improve his softball game as well as his writing, and Louis develops a close yet professional relationship with him. He can't understand why everyone in town objects and acts like it must be a point of scandal that Mr. Forster might be gay. (G)

Keywords: classic; historical setting

Bildner, Phil.

Playing the Field. **Simon & Schuster, 2006.** **S**

The girls' softball team, which has a losing record, is star pitcher Darcy's idea of Hell. She's surprised when her principal, who is dating her mother, gives her a spot on the team. Then she learns there's a catch: Her crush Brandon, the principal's son, has told his dad that Darcy is a lesbian. To play on the team, she'll have to maintain the lie, try to ignore the stigma of being a lesbian, and join the school's gay–straight alliance. The only threat to Darcy's spot on the baseball team is her gay friend Josh, who knows she's straight. (G, Q)

Blacker, Terrence.

Boy2Girl. **Farrar, Straus & Giroux, 2005.** **M** **J**

When Sam's mother dies, he moves from California to England to live with relatives. His cousin Matt dares him to show up at his new school dressed as a girl, a dare that Sam (who poses as Samantha at school) extends for some time. Samantha is a hit; she even draws the eye of the most popular boy in school. The question is: How long can Sam maintain the charade? Although Sam is not transgender, readers who do not question their own gender identity could read this to better understand gender identity and roles. (Q)

Keywords: humor

Block, Francesca Lia.

Weetzie Bat series.

Weetzie Bat. HarperCollins, 1989. **S**

High school is hell for dreamy, eccentric Weetzie Bat, whose Los Angeles world is a modern fairyland. Her best friend Dirk is gay, and she is single. When Weetzie Bat makes a wish that both of them will find true love, that wish comes true. She and My Secret Agent Lover Man, Dirk, and his boyfriend, Duck, move into a house together and start a family. This genre classic, which presents gay friends and family members with love and sensitivity, will complement most collections. (G)

Witch Baby. HarperCollins 1991. **S**

Witch Baby, with her dark hair and purple eyes, feels that she doesn't fit in with the rest of her glittering, happy family. To express her anger, she plays the drums. More than anything, she wants to know her birth mother, a quest that brings her to a group of Jayne Mansfield groupies. Witch Baby is aware that although there is much cruelty in the world, there is also love and hope. Despite their differences, she learns that her family does appreciate her and her honest way of looking at the world.

Cherokee Bat and the Goat Guys. HarperCollins, 1992. **S**

Weetzie's daughter, Cherokee, shares her mother's blonde hair and sunny personality. When Cherokee's half-sister, Witch Baby, stops eating, Cherokee consults a family friend to find a way to save her. The solution comes in the form of a pair of wings. The magic of the wings finds its way to the rock band that Cherokee and Witch Baby form, The Goat Guys, and the band becomes famous. Fame corrupts the two teen girls, but their unusual family still loves and supports them, even as they rebel.

Missing Angel Juan. HarperCollins, 1995. **S**

Miles and mountains can't keep Witch Baby from her true love, Angel Juan. After he leaves for New York to make a living as a musician, Witch Baby is determined to bring Angel Juan back to her home in Los Angeles. In New York, a city with a lot less glitter than her native LA, she finds clues that tell her Angel Juan is in trouble. With magic and love, Witch Baby is able to save Angel Juan, but before that, she meets her grandfather's spirit, which guides her in her quest.

Baby Be-Bop. HarperTrophy, 1997. **S**

Readers travel back in the <u>Weetzie Bat</u> timeline to see Dirk as a teenager. Dirk spends a fairy-tale childhood with his grandmother, Fifi, who in *Weetzie Bat* left her house to Dirk. His teenage years are less than perfect, however, when Dirk feels that he has to hide his homosexuality from the people he loves. After a beating, Dirk isn't sure that he has a reason to live, until he is visited by the spirits of family members. They reassure him that they love him regardless of his sexuality.

Chbosky, Stephen.

🌳 *The Perks of Being a Wallflower.* **MTV Books, 1999.** **S**

In this modern YA classic, letters to an imaginary friend chronicle Charlie's life in high school. All at once Charlie is funny, scared, intelligent, and naïve, observing his world with both passion and ambivalence. High school opens Charlie to new friendships when he drifts away from his old ones. His two closest friends are Sam and Patrick, who help him through times of depression. Near the end of the book Charlie reveals a secret about his Aunt Helen, and facing a dark secret in his past helps him on the road to recovering from trauma. (G)

Awards/honors: BBYA

Cohn, Rachel.

🎗 *Pop Princess*. Simon & Schuster, 2004. **J** **S**

As a child, Wonder Blake was part of a Boston variety show and an aspiring dancer, along with her sister, Lucky. Since Lucky's death, she's done her best to fade away from her local child stardom, a plan that is foiled when a record producer hears her singing at her job at a Dairy Queen. She is mentored by her sister's former best friend, and eventually singing and dancing land Wonder a top 40 hit. In the meantime, Wonder learns that her sister's singing career was full of secrets, including her being a lesbian. (L)

Awards/honors: PPYA

Dole, Mayra Lazara.

🎗 *Down to the Bone*. HarperTeen, 2008. **S**

Laura Amores, a Cuban American resident of Miami, is expelled from her Catholic high school after she is caught reading a love letter from another girl. Her mother cannot accept her as a lesbian either and throws her out of the house. She meets other gay Cuban American teens and moves in with a kind friend and her family. Before she can love and accept anyone else and form a family of people who care about her, Laura must learn to love and accept herself and her sexuality. (L)

Awards/honors: BBYA

Donoghue, Emma.

Stir-Fry. Harper, 1994. **S** **A/YA**

Dublin is the setting for Maria's (rhymes with pariah) freshman year at university, rife with the usual confusion and adjustments to a new environment. When she catches her two female roommates in a kiss, she decides to keep living with them anyway, and they become her advisors and confidantes. Their comfort in their own sexuality leads Maria to think about her own desires. For the first time in her life, Maria gets to decide what Maria likes and wants, and with the help of a friend, she begins to explore her relationship possibilities. (L, Q)

Emberlee, Michelle.

Manstealing for Fat Girls. Soft Skull Press, 2006. **S**

Angie is quirky, smart, and totally not in love with her life, except for her friends Shelby, an out lesbian, and Heather, who only has one developed breast. Her classmates have called her "Lezzylard" since seventh grade. Her overly strict mother is marrying the skanky Rudy. When Angie is sexually assaulted by a popular girl's boyfriend after she tells off the popular girl, Shelby's sister helps them plot revenge. Through crash diets, weird sexual fantasies, and loyal friendships, Angie begins to take a different view of herself. (L)

Flinn, Alex.

Diva. Harper, 2006. **J** **S**

Caitlin, a promising opera singer first seen in Flinn's *Breathing Underwater* (Harper, 2001), auditions for and is accepted by the Miami High School for the Performing Arts. At her new school she makes the closest friends she's had in a long time and develops a crush on Sean, a fellow singer. Sean is gay and dating a boy seriously, but he and Caitlin become good friends. Sean and Caitlin's friendship is just one of several story lines in the book, which also has themes of mother–daughter relationships and commitment to developing one's skills. (G)

Geerling, Marjetta.

Fancy White Trash. Viking, 2008. **J** **S**

Fifteen-year-old Abigail knows exactly what not to do to fall in love with the right guy. Soap operas and her pregnant older sisters have taught her almost everything she needs to know about romance. She has devised a plan for finding her One True Love, and her best friend, Cody, will help her figure it out. Cody is gay but isn't yet out to anyone, even Abigail, a plotline that develops alongside Abigail's soap-opera family life. Abby's plan for finding true love is nearly foiled by the appearance of Cody's older brother, who might be the father of her sister's child. (G)

Keywords: humor

Goldman, Steven.

Two Parties, One Tux, and a Very Short Film About **The Grapes of Wrath**. Bloomsbury, 2008. **M** **J**

Everyday high school life gets a satirical twist. Mitchell is content with his social status of "anonymous nerd." His senior year takes a turn for the ridiculous when his best friend David comes out to him at lunch. Though Mitchell supports David, he wonders if David's coming out will change the dynamics of their friendship. Then Mitchell finds himself catapulted to infamy when he turns in a controversial short film for English about a book he hasn't read and a popular girl wants to date him. (G)

Keywords: humor

Hall, John.

Is He or Isn't He? HarperTeen, 2006. **J** **S**

Best friends and savvy, wealthy New Yorkers Paige and Anthony have made a vow: They'll both have boyfriends by the senior prom. Enter Max. Neither Paige nor Anthony quite knows what to make of Max, sexuality-wise, so they come up with a series of "tests" to see whether he's the type to fall for Paige or Anthony. Can you tell a person's sexuality by the contents of his bedroom? By taking him shopping? By inviting him for a night in a hot tub? This work is cheery and a little predictable, but could work for readers who prefer lighter fare. (G)

Hartinger, Brent.

Split Screen: Attack of the Soul-Sucking Brain Zombies/Bride of the Soul-Sucking Brain Zombies. **HarperTeen, 2007.** **J** **S**

Russel and Min from *Geography Club* (see under "GLBTQ Identity" in chapter 1) and *Order of the Poison Oak* (see under "Teen Romance" in this chapter) tell their stories together in flip-book format. Both have signed up to be extras in a horror film, but they're finding that romance might be just as scary as soul-sucking brain zombies. Russel's ex turns up and wants him back, even though Russel is happy with his current boyfriend. Min hates being alone, but she can't decide if she's lonely enough to pursue a relationship with Leah, who won't come out. Readers will see the same series of events interpreted in two very different ways. (G, L, B)

Keywords: alternative format

Hite, Sid.

The King of Slippery Falls. **Scholastic, 2004.** **M** **J**

"Life is a strange journey," Lewis's eighty-eight-year-old friend Maple tells him. Avid fisherman Lewis's life in Slippery Falls, Idaho, definitely takes a turn for the strange. Just before his sixteenth birthday Lewis, who is adopted, learns that he might be descended from King Louis XV and Madame de Pompadour of France. He shares his discoveries with his best friend and unrequited love interest, Amanda, and worries that their mutual friend Gaston is also interested in Amanda. After a near-fatal accident, however, he learns that Gaston is gay. (G)

Howe, James.

🏵 *The Misfits.* **Atheneum, 2001.** **M** **J**

Dan, Addie, Skeezie, and Joe (or JoDan, or sometimes Scorpio) call themselves "The Gang of Five." Although they are very comfortable with and loyal to each other, they are often teased at school for being different from their peers. Addie is an academic overachiever, Skeezie dresses and acts like someone out of a Mario Puzo novel, Dan is overweight, and Joe is openly gay. At school election time, they know it's time for a change, and Addie runs for office on the No-Name platform, which encourages everyone in the school to look past the labels they give people and abstain from name-calling. (G)

Awards/honors: PPYA

🏵 *Totally Joe.* **Atheneum, 2005.** **M** **J**

Joe from *The Misfits* gets his own story. For an English assignment, he has to write an "alphabiography," a chronicle of his life, with one story for every letter of the alphabet. "C" is for Colin, who is popular, cool, and secretly Joe's boyfriend. Colin isn't as comfortable with his sexuality as Joe is, and definitely is not ready to come out to his classmates. Along with his Colin problems, Joe's is worried about his favorite aunt moving from his hometown to New York City and about Kevin the bully, who incessantly calls him derogatory names. This is an upbeat if slightly unrealistic novel; Joe's wisdom is not always believable, but his strength of character is to be admired. (G)

Awards/honors: ALA Notable Books

Juby, Susan.

Another Kind of Cowboy. **HarperCollins, 2007.** 🇯 🇸

Horses are Alex's calling. His father envisions him as a cowboy, but Alex's interest is dressage, a more artistic endeavor than standard competitive riding. In dressage competition he meets Cleo O'Shea, who is privileged and neglected. Her whose parents have enrolled her at an equestrian boarding school whose students are reputed to have too much money and not enough discipline. The two become friends despite their different personalities. Alex knows he's gay, but he's not yet out to anyone but himself. During his dressage training, Alex also interacts with two instructors, Fergus and Ivan, who are gay. (G)

Katcher, Brian.

Almost Perfect. **Delacorte, 2009.** 🇸

Logan, a senior in high school, is ready to spend his final semester brooding over his recent breakup with his girlfriend of three years. The one person who can lift him out of his funk is new girl Sage Hendricks. Sage and Logan's friendship takes a twist when Logan tries to kiss her and she runs from him. Logan learns that Sage harbors an unusual secret: She's a boy. His reaction to her news is unkind, but it paves the way for Logan to achieve a deeper understanding of Sage's identity as well as his own. (T)

Koertge, Ron.

Boy Girl Boy. **Harcourt, 2005.** 🇯 🇸

Elliot, Theresa, and Larry are the tightest literary trio since Harry, Hermione, and Ron. They're planning to move from their small town to glamorous California when they're done with high school, living happily as best friends, but as the book goes on, they each start to wonder about their lives outside their closest friends. Larry thinks he might be gay. Theresa wants other boys in her world. Elliot wonders what he'd be like on his own, unencumbered by what everyone else thinks of him. Told in three individual voices, with lots of fast dialogue and humor. (G, Q)

Keywords: alternative format

Korman, Gordon.

Born to Rock. **Hyperion, 2006.** 🇯 🇸

Conservative Leo is on his way to Harvard, until he is accused of cheating on a test. When he loses his scholarship, he dedicates his summer to working as a roadie for his biological father's punk band, Purge. Following Leo and Purge on the road are Leo's two closest friends, Owen and Melinda. Leo is so caught up in his own worries about college and getting to know his biological father that he ignores many messages his friends are trying to tell him. Leo does not even realize Owen is gay until the end of the book, although hints are dropped throughout the text. (G)

Keywords: humor

Krovatin, Christopher.

Venomous. **Atheneum, 2008.** **S**

Anger isn't just a problem for Locke Venetti; it's an entity that he refers to as "the venom." More and more, the venom seems to take him over quickly, with great violence. Via his friend Randall, Locke makes a new friend, Casey, who understands how Locke feels when the venom rages. When they first meet, Casey believes that Locke is gay and kisses him. They fight over their misunderstanding, but eventually become friends. Through Casey, Locke meets his girlfriend and a new circle of friends. (G)

Levithan, David.

Wide Awake. **Knopf, 2006.** **S**

As in *Boy Meets Boy* (see the "Teen Romance" section, below), the characters in this book live in a gay-friendly alternate reality and speak with warmth and humor. After battles and wars, the United States is run by a group of Jesus devotees who believe in love and equality for all. A gay Jewish man, Abe Stein, is elected president of the United States, but when his election is challenged, Duncan Weiss, also gay and Jewish, travels to Topeka, Kansas, with boyfriend Jimmy to protest the challenge. Their travels change their outlook on activism and politics. (G, L)

Keywords: alternate reality; fantasy

Lockhart, E.

Dramarama. **Random House, 2007.** **J** **S**

Sarah, aka Sadye, is straight and white, and her best friend Douglas, aka Demi, is gay and African American. What brings them together is their mutual love of theater, specifically musical theater, and they are excited to be attending the same summer drama camp. Although the multitalented Demi becomes a star at camp and finds romance, Sadye's talent falls short of that of most of her campmates. Their separation by talent takes a toll on their friendship, and Sadye, frustrated by the camp musical director, is faced with the choice of saving her reputation or Demi's potential career. (G)

Fly on the Wall: How One Girl Saw Everything. **Delacorte, 2006 .** **S**

Kafka gets an update and a little twist. Gretchen Yee, an artist who attends a school in Manhattan where everyone is "talented" and "special," wishes that she could become a fly on the wall of the boys' locker room. Her wish is granted, and for a week as a fly, she observes teen male bodies and behaviors. Gretchen discovers that her ex-boyfriend has a cruel streak, and her crush Titus reveals that his father is gay. Gretchen's metamorphosis is funny and revealing, and she becomes a better person for her experience. (G)

Keywords: fantasy; humor

Malloy, Brian.

Twelve Long Months. **Scholastic, 2008. S**

Molly has a huge crush on Mark, the cutest, broodiest boy in her boring town in Minnesota. When they're assigned to be lab partners, the two become friends, and when Molly learns they're both headed to New York City after graduation, she is convinced they're destined to be together. That belief crumbles when she learns that Mark is gay. However, instead of breaking apart, Molly and Mark's friendship grows stronger. All may not be well in their friendship, though, when Molly's boyfriend Simon needs a roommate and she volunteers Mark. (G)

Marino, Peter.

Magic and Misery. **Holiday House, 2009. S**

T.J. (short for Tony Jo) has never, to her dismay, had a boyfriend. However, she has a strong bond of friendship with Pan (short for the nickname Pansy; his real name is James), who came out to their class. When T.J. starts dating smart, not-wholly-unpopular football player Caspar, their three-way friendship causes trouble for all of them. T.J. feels that Pan isn't being a good friend to her when she needs him most, and Pan and Caspar are jealous of each other. (G)

Matthews, Andrew.

The Flip Side. **Delacorte, 2003. J S**

Robert is thrilled to have landed the role of Rosalind in his school's performance of *As You Like It* because his crush, Milena, is playing Orlando. During the course of rehearsals and performance, Robert learns he enjoys dressing up in women's clothing and performing his female role. His classmates discuss gender roles in their English classes, and one of them throws a cross-dressing party. Fascinated by gender-bending, Robert even shares a kiss with Milena, but he decides that he is not gay even as his best friend Kev comes out to him. (G, Q)

Mowry, Jess.

Babylon Boyz. **Simon & Schuster, 1997. J S**

Dante, Pook, and Wyatt are faced with a dilemma: They've found a suitcase full of cocaine and can't decide whether to flush it, which they know to be the right thing to do, or to sell it and make some desperately needed money. Life for the three boys in the Babylon section of Oakland is rough, and they all have their own issues to deal with in addition to daily racism, violence, and poverty. Dante was born with a bad heart. Pook, who is gay, wants to attend medical school. Wyatt, an aspiring photographer, lives to eat. (G)

Keywords: urban fiction

Murdock, Catherine Gilbert.

Dairy Queen trilogy.

🏆 *Dairy Queen.* **Houghton Mifflin, 2006. J S**

Football is the way out of a submissive life running the family farm for high school junior D.J. Schwenk. While training the quarterback from the rival high school's team and making the decision to go out for football herself, she notices that her best friend Amber isn't herself. Amber confesses that she is in love with D.J., who has never known a gay person. Although this is D.J.'s story, Amber's lesbianism is one of a few important plot points, and it plays a central role in the sequel. (L)

Awards/honors: BBYA

🎗 *The Off Season.* Houghton Mifflin, 2007. **J S**

D.J. Schwenk is back, and for once her life is going pretty well. She's playing linebacker on her school's football team and making passing grades. Her best friend Amber, however, is being bullied at school because she's dating another girl. Amber decides to drop out of high school and run away with her girlfriend rather than face the daily harassment. In defending Amber, D.J. is barred from playing football. D.J. has to put her sports and personal life in perspective, though, when her older brother suffers a near-fatal, debilitating injury while playing college football. (L)

Awards/honors: BBYA

Keywords: bullying

Front and Center. Houghton Mifflin, 2009. **J S**

It's winter in Wisconsin, which means it's finally time for D.J.'s favorite sport: basketball. This book mostly focuses on D.J.'s college decision, as she's already being scouted by Big Ten schools, but she doesn't give up her friendship with Amber, either. Amber and her girlfriend, barbecue maven Dale, are still together and happy. Due to in-school bullying, however, Amber only shows up at school to attend classes. Her absence saddens D.J., who finds herself caught not only between two schools, but between two boys. In the end, though, Amber is there for D.J. when D.J. needs her most. (L)

Keywords: bullying

Murray, Martine.

The Slightly True Story of Cedar B. Hartley, Who Planned to Live an Unusual Life. Scholastic, 2003. **M**

Twelve-year-old Cedar's outlook on her Australian neighborhood, rather than her life, is unusual. She's never known her father (who, according to her mother, died of a heart attack), and her older brother ran away from home and keeps in touch only with postcards. Cedar befriends Kite, a boy her age whose parents are circus performers. Kite teaches Cedar acrobatics, and their friendship evolves into a romance. It is Kite who helps Cedar realize that she has a gift for understanding people. Among Cedar's eccentric neighbors are a male couple, who adopt a baby. (G)

Myracle, Lauren.

Kissing Kate. Dutton, 2003. **J** **S**

At a party, high school juniors and best friends Lissa and Kate share a kiss, but the kiss leads to anger and confusion rather than a romance. Kate, the beautiful, popular one with a boyfriend, avoids Lissa at school, leaving Lissa to deal with the fallout from the kiss on her own. Since her parents' death Lissa lacks an older female role model, but her offbeat coworker Ariel provides distraction, humor, and most important, a listening ear. Ariel becomes Lissa's confidante, and because of Ariel Lissa gains the strength she needs to express her feelings about her sexuality. (L, B, Q)

Naylor, Phyllis Reynolds.

Alice on the Outside. Atheneum, 1999. **M** **J**

Eighth grade is full of questions for Alice, in this eleventh book in the <u>Alice</u> series. She and her best friends, Pamela and Elizabeth, realize they'll be spending the summer mostly apart from each other, and a social experiment at school that separates dark-haired and fair-haired students to teach them about discrimination teaches Alice that prejudice is still alive and well. A new friend, Lori, is a lesbian, and is interested in Alice. Despite Alice's strictly platonic feelings for her friend, she handles the situation with grace and an open mind. There are currently twenty-three titles in the <u>Alice</u> series. (L)

Keywords: series fiction

Nelson, Blake.

Girl. Simon & Schuster, 1994. **S**

As her high school years progress, Andrea shifts from suburban mall rat to follower of underground bands who wears the coolest vintage clothes. Andrea is introduced to the music scene by her friend Cybil, who is the lead singer in a band that gains local fame. Cybil introduces Andrea to Todd Sparrow, who becomes Andrea's on-and-off boyfriend. Throughout the book, Cybil and Andrea alternately stay close and grow apart, but Andrea always admires Cybil, who comes out to Andrea as a lesbian late in the book. (G, L)

Papademetriou, Lisa, and Chris Tebbetts.

M or F? Razorbill, 2005. **J** **S**

Marcus and Frannie are best friends who describe themselves as "brain twins." Frannie has a crush on the new boy, Jeff, but doesn't have the courage to ask him out or even talk to him much directly at school. She communicates with him through chat rooms, where Marcus, who is gay, plays her Cyrano: She hands the keyboard over to him, and he entices Jeff with wit and wisdom. Eventually Marcus starts talking to Jeff on his own behalf, and this strains his friendship with Frannie. The story is told through alternating viewpoints. (G)

Keywords: humor

Peters, Julie Anne.

Far from Xanadu. Little, Brown, 2005. **S**

Mike (nickname for Mary Elizabeth) is a butch, out lesbian in a small Kansas town. Xanadu is the new girl, sent out of the city when she was caught dealing drugs. Mike falls hard for Xanadu and is determined to date her, but Xanadu is straight, and Mike has a hard time dealing with Xanadu's dating boys. Normally confident in who she is, Mike takes Xanadu's rejection hard, turning to drinking to cope. Eventually she realizes that she will have to leave her accepting community to pursue a loving relationship. (G, L)

Plum-Ucci, Carol.

What Happened to Lani Garver. Harcourt, 2002. **J** **S**

Lani Garver's arrival on Hackett Island causes quite a stir among the island's teens, especially popular Claire McKenzie. On the island, being different is a sin, and Lani Garver is more different than anyone Claire or her friends have ever met. Lani's androgynous style raises the same question from everyone: Is Lani a boy or a girl? As Claire and Lani interact and grow closer, and events from Lani's past come to light, Claire is forced to confront some of her own identity issues, including the causes behind her battle with leukemia. (G, Q)

Revoyr, Nina.

🏵 *The Necessary Hunger*. St. Martin's Press, 1998. **S**

Basketball is the catalyst for Japanese American Nancy's crush on Raina Webber. Nancy meets Raina through her father, who is dating Raina's mother despite criticism from their friends. Nancy finds Raina confident and strong, something she doesn't feel about herself, and soon becomes sexually as well as emotionally involved with Raina. Raina plays basketball for a school in a different league from Nancy's, and the two have a final face-off in a league game. The girls live in a dangerous place, but the author refrains from making their environment a major issue. (L)

Awards/honors: PPYA

Reynolds, Marilyn.

Love Rules. True-to-Life Series from Hamilton High No. 8. Morning Glory Press, 2001. **J** **S**

Lynn's best friend Kit has spent the summer in San Francisco, and Lynn can't wait to hear about it. Kit opens up to Lynn and comes out to her as a lesbian, and although Lynn is surprised, she is supportive. Using another high school's model, Kit attempts to start a gay–straight alliance at her school, which is not exactly friendly to GLBT students. While bold Kit reveals her sexuality to all by shaving her head, Lynn deals with issues of her own when she starts dating an African American football player. There are nine titles in the <u>True-to-Life Series from Hamilton High</u>. (L)

Keywords: series fiction; urban fiction

Roth, Matthue.

🏵 *Never Mind the Goldbergs.* **Scholastic, 2005.** 🅂

Hava Aaronson is an unorthodox Orthodox Jew. She loves the traditions of Judaism but has her own punk-rock take on long skirts. An aspiring actress, she is thrilled to land a role on a TV sitcom about an Orthodox Jewish family. Hollywood's view of Judaism is very different than her own, and Hava faces a lot of challenges on the set of her show (including getting kosher food from craft service). Hava's best friends, who guide her through the craziness that is showbiz, are Moishe, a filmmaker, and Ben, who is gay and not Jewish. (G)

Awards/honors: PPYA

Ruditis, Paul.

Rainbow Party. **Simon Pulse, 2005.** 🅂

This controversial novel follows thirteen invitees of a "rainbow party," at which each girl wears a different color lipstick and the boys drop their pants. Gin, the hostess, who takes pride in being able to please a boy, is worried that no one will come. Monogamous, devoted couple Ash and Rose don't think they're ready to have oral sex in front of other people. Hunter and Perry are no strangers to oral sex, performing it in the school bathroom, but Perry is a lot more interested in Hunter than Hunter is in him. (G)

Ryan, Sara.

The Rules for Hearts: A Family Drama. **Viking, 2007.** 🅂

Battle Hall Davies, first seen in *Empress of the World* (see under "GLBTQ Identity" in chapter 1), travels from North Carolina to Oregon the summer before her freshman year at Reed College. What she doesn't tell her parents is that she'll be living with her estranged brother, Nick, who ran away from home four years ago; their parents believe he is in New York City. She and Nick live in Forest House, whose creative inhabitants stage a production of *A Midsummer Night's Dream.* At Forest House, Battle begins a relationship with another housemate, Meryl, who Battle suspects has a history with Nick. (L)

Sanchez, Alex.

Getting It. **Simon & Schuster, 2006.** 🄼 🄹 🅂

"Typical fifteen-year-old boy" is a perfect description for Carlos Amoroso, who wants a date with popular hottie Roxy Rodriguez. Inspired by *Queer Eye for the Straight Guy,* Carlos asks stylish gay classmate Sal to give him a makeover. Sal consents on one condition: Carlos has to help him form a gay–straight alliance at school. This request is a source of consternation for Carlos: Will his friends think he's gay? In the course of their friendship, Carlos learns much about confidence, grooming, and style as Sal's makeover gives him the strength to confront his homophobic father and classmates. Sanchez uses humor and realistic dialogue to easily cover some important, heavy topics. (G)

Rainbow Boys Trilogy.

The last two books complete the trilogy and chronicle the end of Jason, Kyle, and Nelson's high school careers. Though Jason and Kyle's relationship is an important plotline, the overarching story is about the friendship among the three boys and the ways they bond over their shared sexuality.

Rainbow Boys. Annotated under "Teen Romance," below.

🦋 *Rainbow High.* Simon & Schuster, 2003. **S**

This second book in the Rainbow Boys trilogy finds Jason questioning whether he should come out to his fellow basketball players; Kyle debating whether he should attend Princeton, which would mean leaving Jason behind; and Nelson in a relationship with Jeremy, who is HIV positive. Eventually, Jason does come out on public television, but he pays for his honesty and his love for Kyle with the loss of his basketball scholarship. The boys support each other as their high school graduation approaches. (G)

Awards/honors: BBYA

Rainbow Road. Simon & Schuster, 2005. **S**

Nelson, Kyle, and Jason, last seen in *Rainbow High*, are taking a road trip from Virginia to California, where Jason has been invited to speak at a new GLBT high school about his experiences coming out. While traveling to California, they meet a diverse cast of GLBT characters, including a male-to-female transgender and a gay couple who have been together for twenty years. Nelson's lack of character development may bother some readers, but Kyle's questioning of his relationship with bisexual Jason makes up for it. As in the other two books in the trilogy, the boys remain loyal to each other even through their disagreements. (G, L, B, T)

Sloan, Brian.

A Tale of Two Summers. **Simon & Schuster, 2006. S**

Hal, who is gay, and Chuck, who is straight, have been best friends for ten years and are spending their first summer apart. Rather than share a pair of pants (like the Sisterhood of the Traveling Pants group), they set up a private blog so they can communicate. They talk at least once a day, sharing adventures and exploits. At camp, Hal meets sexy bohemian pot smoker Henri, and Chuck meets Ghaliyah, a singer who is cast opposite him in the camp play. Through the blog Hal and Chuck talk honestly and humorously about sex and relationships. (G)

Swados, Elizabeth.

Flamboyant. **Picador, 1998. S A/YA**

Orthodox Jew Chana Landau feels like a gefilte fish out of water when she takes a job teaching at Harvey Milk High in Manhattan, an alternative high school for gay and lesbian students. Though her religion dictates that homosexuality is an abomination, she keeps an open mind and heart and even earns the respect of her students by maintaining a calm demeanor. The book is told via diary entries in alternating points of view between Chana and Flamboyant, a smart fifteen-year-old boy who supports a drug habit by turning tricks on the West Side Highway. (G, L, Q)

Keywords: alternative format

Sweeney, Joyce.

Face the Dragon. **Delacorte, 1992.** **J** **S**

Fourteen-year-old best friends Eric and Paul participate in an accelerated program at their high school. For years, Eric has been the follower to Paul's leader. A class reading of *Beowulf* inspires Eric to face his own dragons, which makes him increasingly more competitive and independent. This independence, however, spirals into a constant need to compete against Paul. Paul reveals to Eric his thoughts that he might be gay, and when an evil teacher threatens to expose Paul's sexuality, Eric has to put his competitiveness aside. (G)

Taylor, William.

Jerome. **Alyson Publications, 1999.** **S**

As this novel opens, Jerome dies, and his suicide brings together two of his closest friends, Kate and Marco. Kate, an exchange student in the United States, trades letters with Marco, who is still at home in New Zealand. As they discuss Jerome, Kate, whom Marco has always known as Jerome's girlfriend, confesses to Marco that Jerome is gay, she's a lesbian, and they posed as each other's boyfriend and girlfriend to escape persecution by their peers. She also reveals that one of the reasons behind Jerome's suicide was an unrequited crush on Marco. (G, L)

Torres, Lisa.

November Ever After. **Holiday House, 1999.** **S**

Amy's small world seems to grow even smaller after her mother dies. Her father, a pastor, is too caught up in his own mourning and in counseling his churchgoers to see how lonely Amy is. Amy depends on her best (and only) friend Sara, who has been spending time with Anita. After learning that Sara and Anita are in a romantic relationship, Amy has many questions that go along with her increased feelings of isolation. Will people think she's a lesbian, too? What do her religious beliefs say about maintaining a friendship with Sara? (L)

Watts, Julia.

Finding H.F. **Alyson Books, 2001.** **J** **S**

Morgan, Kentucky, in the Appalachian Bible belt, is not the most friendly environment for gay and lesbian teens. Heavenly Faith, H.F. for short, was named by her grandmother in the hope that she would lead a more traditional, "normal" life than did her mother, who abandoned her. After her sophomore year, H.F. and her best friend Bo, who is teased because he is not stereotypically masculine, put their money together, get in Bo's Ford Escort, and travel to Florida in hopes of finding H.F.'s mother. Along the way, they discover themselves as well as the American South. (L)

Wieler, Diana.

🏆 *Bad Boy*. Delacorte, 1992. **J** **S**

Ice hockey is known for being an aggressive sport, and A.J. is known for being an aggressive player, whom his coach employs to take cheap shots against other players. A.J. experiences even more personal confusion when he learns that his friend Tulsa is gay. Rather than talk about his feelings, he channels his anger and feelings of betrayal into violence on the ice. To further complicate things, A.J. falls for Tulsa's sister. In his development as a character, A.J. questions masculinity and sexuality. (G, Q)

Awards/honors: BBYA

Williams, Bett.

Girl Walking Backwards. St. Martin's Griffin, 1998. **S**

Cynical, mostly out lesbian Skye is dealing all at once with a new school, a New Age–crazed mother, and her friend Jessica, who introduces Skye to a world of raves and drugs. Jessica, unfortunately, is more a reflection of Skye's mother than a stand-alone friend; she is unstable and volatile, although her instability leads Skye to see that she must face the dysfunctional people in her own life rather than avoid them. Skye's sexuality here is nuanced, never black-and-white, and her friends and family are multidimensional. The lack of easy answers and neat endings gives this book a gritty, realistic touch. (L)

Withrow, Sarah.

What Gloria Wants. Groundwood, 2005. **J** **S**

The ugly world of teenage sexual politics plays out here. After Gloria sprains her ankle in front of Marc's house, the two of them start dating. Marc is lusted after at school but is terrible boyfriend material, domineering and even abusive. Marc's relationship with his friend Hamish is hardly normal, either; he allows Hamish to watch him making out with Gloria. Gloria's frenemy Shawna is jealous after Gloria gets Marc for herself and becomes best friends with Tina. In the course of their triangular friendship, Tina reveals to Gloria in confidence that she is a lesbian. (L)

Wittlinger, Ellen.

🏆 *What's in a Name?*. Simon & Schuster, 2000. **J**

Ten distinct narrators tell a story about a debate over a town's name, and each of the ten narrators' opinions about what the town name should be parallels their thoughts about themselves and how others see them. The wealthier residents would prefer that the name of the town be changed from "Scrub Harbor" to the more genteel "Folly Bay." O'Neill decides during the debate to come out as gay via a public display of poetry, and his brother the jock has to think about how their connection affects him. (G)

Awards/honors: BBYA

Keywords: alternative format

Yamanaka, Lois Ann.

🎗 *Name Me Nobody*. **Hyperion, 1999.** **J**

Emi-Lou, raised by her grandmother since the age of three when her mother ran off to California, is teased at school because of her weight and her friendship with Von Vierra, who is thought to be a lesbian because of her butch style. Von joins a women's softball team, and Emi-Lou, desperate to follow her, goes on a diet to make the team. Once they're both on the team, though, Von hangs out more with another girl on the team, and the two begin dating. Emi-Lou then attracts two male volleyball players, but girls at school tell her the boys are only out for one thing. (L)

Awards/honors: PPYA

Family

A family doesn't have to be dysfunctional to make for a great story. Families and the role they play in teens' lives often determine how comfortable a GLBTQ teen feels coming out. Books in this section fall into two categories: those told from the point of view of straight teens who have gay family members, and those about gay teens within the context of their families. The major difference between these books and the books in the section on GLBTQ identity is tone. These books are usually lighter and often incorporate humor. The families in these books have loving, if imperfect, relationships.

Bechard, Margaret.

If It Doesn't Kill You. **Viking, 1999.** **J** **S**

Freshman year is rarely easy, and as far as Ben's concerned, he's got quite enough problems. His football team might be the worst one to ever exist. He can't seem to get the hang of driving. The last thing Ben needs is his father, whose high school football days are the stuff of legend, telling him and his mother that he's gay and leaving them to live with his new partner. Ben's jock friends are definitely not gay friendly, and Ben would rather ignore the situation entirely, figuring his father's sexuality is his prerogative. (G)

Burch, Christian.

The Manny Files. **Atheneum, 2006.** **M**

Mary Poppins comes to eight-year-old Keats's family in the form of his new male nanny, or "manny." Keats's gay manny brings a sense of style as well as a little melodrama to the family, and Keats is not your everyday eight-year-old; he is fashion conscious and wise. His older sister Lulu is not pleased with the manny's behavior and starts to document his actions in a journal. Lulu confronts the manny in a family meeting, and Keats, who is inspired by the manny to embrace his own differences, rushes to his defense. (G)

Hit the Road, Manny: A Manny Files Novel. **(Sequel). Atheneum, 2008.** **M**

Keats is expecting an iPod for his birthday. Not only does he not get the iPod, his family announces on his birthday that they're taking a road trip. The entire family, including the manny, gets into the new RV and travels west. The one moment of the road trip that isn't so fun is a stop in the manny's hometown. Despite the love and warmth that the manny brings to Keats's family, the manny's own family doesn't accept him or his fabulousness. (G)

Cohn, Rachel.

[Cyd Charisse].

🎗 *Gingerbread.* Simon & Schuster, 2002. **M** **J**

After being kicked out of boarding school, rule breaker Cyd Charisse is sent back to San Francisco to live with her mom and stepdad. When she breaks their rules, they ship her out to New York to live with her biological father and stepsiblings and work at her gay half-brother's coffee bar. Despite her defiant nature, which leads to conflicts with her stepsiblings, Cyd begins to learn what it's like to be part of a family; her New York family opens her heart to being more honest with her San Francisco family. (G)

Awards/honors: BBYA

Shrimp. Simon & Schuster, 2005.

Cupcake. Simon & Schuster, 2007.

Coy, John.

Crackback. **Scholastic, 2005.** **J** **S**

Football player Miles looks forward to a great season, until his coach resigns. Coach's replacement runs the football team like a dictatorship, and Miles is quickly losing his love of the game. At the same time, an assignment involving his family tree strains his relationship with his father. His uncle, who is gay, holds the key to Miles's completing his assignment, but his homophobic father expresses anger and resentment when Miles says he wants to contact his uncle. Other topics touched upon in this book include steroid use, abuse of power and authority, and budding romance. (G)

D'Erasmo, Stacey.

A Seahorse Year. **Houghton Mifflin, 2004.** **A/YA**

Sixteen-year-old runaway Christopher has a somewhat unusual family life. His mother Nan is in a long-term relationship with another woman, and his sperm-donor father Hal, a dancer turned accountant, is gay. Christopher himself is schizophrenic and has undergone several unsuccessful treatments. By shifting viewpoints, the author tells the story of Christopher's conception, Nan's abusive childhood, and Hal's search for love. Christopher's mental illness serves as a catalyst for a story that is more about change and identity than about the illness itself. (G, L)

Durant, Penny.

When Heroes Die. Simon & Schuster, 1992. **M** **J**

Since Gary's father abandoned the family when Gary was born, his uncle Rob has been his guide and father figure. Gary is crushed when his mother tells him that Rob has AIDS and is dying. Just before Rob dies, he reveals to Gary that he is gay. Gary wonders if he might be gay, too, due to his discomfort around girls, and Rob helps him put sexuality into perspective. Gary finds little support from his homophobic best friend, but his mother and a few other characters help him through his anger, grief, and denial. (G)

Earls, Nick.

48 Shades of Brown. Graphia, 2004 (paperback reprint). **S**

When his parents move to Geneva, Switzerland, Dan decides to stay in Brisbane, Australia, to finish his senior year of high school. He moves in with his young Aunt Jacq and her roommate, Naomi. Dan falls for Naomi, who unfortunately has a boyfriend who's a real jerk. With the same enthusiasm he applies to his schoolwork, Dan tries to win Naomi's heart, but he still has quite a bit to learn about love. Near the end, Jacq reveals to Dan that she is a lesbian and that she too is in love with Naomi. (L)

Fox, Paula.

🌟 *The Eagle Kite*. Orchard, 1995. **J**

Liam's father is dying of AIDS. His mother tells him his father got the virus through a blood transfusion, but Liam knows she's lying. His father, Philip, moves to a cabin alone, and it is there during Thanksgiving, when Liam confronts him that Philip reveals his biggest secrets. Philip tells the story of his love, Geoff, whom he never talked about with Liam and his mother. Geoff died of AIDS, and Philip was his caregiver. Although Philip succumbs to AIDS at the end, he dies knowing that Liam knows the truth. (G)

Awards/honors: BBYA

Freymann-Weyr, Garret.

🌟 *My Heartbeat*. Houghton Mifflin, 2002. **J** **S**

Ellen's brother Link and his best friend James are inseparable, and Ellen has an unrequited crush on James. When Ellen, following up on a question asked by a classmate, asks James and Link if they could be described as a couple, Link says no and James says yes. During their strained friendship Ellen begins dating James, who helps her to understand her quiet, avoidant family. The complex relationships and many references to arts and literature make this book an excellent choice for sensitive, thoughtful readers. (G)

Awards/honors: BBYA; Printz honor book

Garden, Nancy.

Holly's Secret. **Farrar, Straus & Giroux, 2000.** **M** **J**

Holly's got a chance for the ultimate makeover: a move from New York to Massachusetts. After a humiliating incident at summer camp, Holly knows that the first thing she has to hide with her makeover is that she's the adopted daughter of a lesbian couple. She models her new identity, "Yvette," as someone glamorous, not into sports, and most important, with a traditional family. Her mothers let her get away with it, but eventually Holly learns that honesty is the best policy when it comes to matters of identity. (L)

Griffin, Adele.

Split Just Right. **Hyperion, 1997.** **M** **J**

For Dandelion, aka Danny's single mother Susan, all the world's a perpetual stage. She's melodramatic off stage, acts in commercials and local theater productions, and teaches at an upscale private school so Danny can attend for free. Danny's primary father figures are her gay upstairs neighbors, Gary and Elliot. Now in ninth grade, Danny has questions about her father, whom she doesn't remember and has never communicated with. She writes him a letter, and in a mix-up Susan reveals that she was not entirely truthful with Danny about their relationship. (G)

Halpin, Brendan.

🏵 *Donorboy.* **Villard, 2004.** **A/YA**

Rosalind was born to a lesbian couple who used donor sperm to achieve pregnancy. When her mothers are killed in a car accident, she is sent to live with her sperm-donor father, Sean Cassidy. Sean has never been a part of Ros's life, and his first foray into parenting is riddled with mistakes. E-mails, journal entries, and text messages unfold the story of how Sean and Ros come to know each other, particularly one event in which Ros assaults a classmate who makes fun of her dead mother and Sean defends her. (L)

Awards/honors: Alex Award winner; BBYA

Harmon, Michael.

🏵 *The Last Exit to Normal.* **Knopf, 2008.** **S**

Three years prior to the start of the book, Ben's father revealed that he was gay. Since then, Ben's been smoking a lot of pot, riding his skateboard nonstop, and doing whatever else he can think of to anger his father. The last thing Ben expects is for his dad to pluck him from the city and move him, with his boyfriend Edward, to Montana. Ben is furious with his father, but the move turns out to be good for him, exposing him to new ways of life and forcing him to lose some of his egocentricity. (G)

Awards/honors: BBYA

Homes, A. M.

🔥 *Jack*. Simon & Schuster, 1989. **J**

Every day, fifteen-year-old Jack works to maintain a façade of normalcy after his parents' divorce. Years after the divorce, Jack's father comes out to him. Jack is angry as well as confused: Could he be homosexual, too? At school, Jack's best friend Max accidentally spills Jack's secret, leading to Jack's being taunted and teased by his peers. Over time Jack sees that having a gay father is not the end of the world, and he rethinks his idea of what "family" means when he learns Max's traditional family is not as perfect as Max makes it seem. (G)

Awards/honors: BBYA

Jenkins, A. M.

Breaking Boxes. Delacorte, 1997. **J** **S**

Since his mother's death, sixteen-year-old Charlie has lived with his twenty-four-year-old brother, Trent. Trent is gay, something Charlie has known since his childhood. Trent keeps quiet about his sexuality to spare Charlie from social ostracism. However, it is Charlie who breaks Trent's silence, telling his new friend Brandon that Trent is gay. Unfortunately Charlie overestimates Brandon's level of tolerance, and Brandon, revolted by Charlie's news, tells their classmates Charlie's secret. Through realistic and sometimes coarse language, Charlie and Brandon repair their friendship despite their differences. (G)

Kerr, M. E.

Deliver Us from Evie. Harper, 1994. **J** **S**

This is a landmark "friends and family" book, narrated by Parr Burman, whose sister Evie doesn't fit the conventions of a traditional female. Parr is thankful for this, because Evie's love of farming means that he won't have to take over the family business. Homophobic attitudes in Parr's small town come to light as Evie begins spending more time with Patsy Duff, the daughter of a prominent resident, despite her mother's attempts to match her with Cord, a farmhand. Social pressure pushes Parr to post a sign, the language on which hurts Evie. (L)

Night Kites. Harper & Row, 1986. **S**

Erick seems to have it all as far as relationships are concerned: a terrific girlfriend and a best friend, Jack. Jack's girlfriend Nicki makes a move on Erick, and Erick, who believes that he and Nicki have a connection besides their relationships to Jack, responds. His romance with Nicki costs him his friendship with Jack as well as his relationship with his girlfriend. At the time Erick struggles with his friendships and romances, his brother Pete, who is his idol, reveals to Erick that he is both gay and HIV positive. (G)

Klein, Norma.

Now That I Know. Bantam, 1988. **M** **J**

Nina lives as normal a life as a joint custody kid can have. Both of her divorced parents still live in Manhattan, and she spends half a week with each parent. She has a close relationship with her father, which changes drastically when her father tells her he's gay and that his partner is moving in with him. After he reveals his secret, Nina is upset with her father and avoids him, and he fears losing her love. At the same time, her flirtatious, sexually aware best friend is encouraging Nina to be more open to her own sexuality. (G)

Koertge, Ron.

🏵 *The Arizona Kid.* **Avon, 1989.** **S**

A summer in Arizona on his Uncle Wes's ranch teaches Billy quite a bit about life and himself. Wes is gay and an AIDS educator, and comfortably speaks with Billy about all the things guys worry about, including safer sex. Over the summer, Billy falls in love with Cara Mae, an equestrian, and considers some options for his future career. Billy handles differences and shortcomings, both his own and other people's, with humor and teenage sophistication. (G)

Awards/honors: BBYA

Madison, Bennett.

The Blonde of the Joke. **HarperCollins, 2009.** **J** **S**

Since her best friends moved away, Val has resigned herself to the role of loner. Then Francie Knight, blonde and brazen, befriends her. Together, Val and Francie engage in a lot of shoplifting. They set out to steal the Holy Grail, their "Most Beautiful Thing," without knowing what it is. As they grow closer, Val reveals that her gay older brother, Jesse, is dying of an illness that is never named in the book. Francie's bold nature inspires Val to visit Jesse in his home in a nearby city, and Val and Jesse rekindle their relationship in the months before his death. (G)

Maguire, Gregory.

Oasis. **Clarion, 1996.** **M** **J**

This family drama revolves around Hand Gunther, who runs a motel with his father, Rudy. When Rudy dies, Hand blames himself, but he is also angry with his mother Clare, who left the family three years before the story opens, for not responding more quickly to the family's emergency. Blinded by guilt and anger, Hand eventually learns to forgive both his mother and himself. The theme of death is supplemented by Emily Dickinson's poetry, a story line about Hand's uncle, and a theater set designer who is dying of AIDS. (G)

Malloy, Brian.

The Year of Ice. **St. Martin's Griffin, 2003.** **S** **A/YA**

Winters are harsh in Minneapolis, and senior Kevin Doyle's secrets are even harsher. First, he's got a huge crush on Jon Thompson. He and Jon are friends, but Jon is as straight as they come and would probably beat Kevin to a pulp if Kevin tried to romance him. Second, he learns that his mother's death may have been a suicide engendered by his father's affair. On the outside, Kevin maintains an air of normalcy, dating a girl and making plans for his life after high school, but as his relationship with his father becomes more strained, he knows he'll have to make some major decisions. (G)

Martin, Ann.

Here Today. **Scholastic, 2004.** **M**

Dramatic, delusional Doris Day Dingman's dream is to be an actress, so she leaves her husband and sixth-grader Ellie to care for her younger brothers and sisters when she moves to New York in 1963. Ellie must act in a parenting role while her father works long hours. Even school is not an escape, because her peers bully her. Ellie's best friend Holly and a lesbian couple are part of her neighborhood family on Witch Tree Lane, and this family helps Emma through tough times and tragic events. (L)

Keywords: classic; historical setting

Na, An.

The Fold. **Penguin, 2008.** **J** **S**

Joyce has always looked up to her sister Helen, who is not only smart, but beautiful. Looks aren't terribly important to Joyce; that is, until her aunt wins the lottery. Joyce's aunt wants to use her lottery winnings to get Joyce surgery to create the folds not seen on Asian eyes. Joyce begins to question what it means to be beautiful, looking to Helen for advice. Although the rest of her family knows Helen's secret, Joyce is one of the last people to be let in on the secret that Helen is a lesbian. (L)

Nelson, Theresa.

Earthshine. **Orchard Books, 1994.** **M** **J** **S**

Slim moves to LA to live with her actor father Mack after her mother's third marriage. What Slim doesn't tell her mother is that her father has AIDS and is just months from dying. In a support group for other children of AIDS victims, Slim finds an auxiliary family. Her anger and grief about her father's illness and her feelings toward his partner Larry are just as strong as her love. Slim, her father, Larry, and a member of her support group, Isaiah, make a pilgrimage to the Hungry Valley, which although it does not provide the cure they were looking for, does give them a new perspective on life. (G)

Paulsen, Gary.

🌳 *The Car.* **Harcourt, 1994.** **M** **J**

Terry's parents have each made the decision to leave their marriage and family. Unfortunately for Terry, they've made that decision at the exact same time, abandoning Terry. Fortunately, Terry has a car kit and the tools needed to put it together, which he does, and then he teaches himself to drive. The novel is reminiscent of Mark Twain's *The Adventures of Huckleberry Finn*; Terry leaves Cleveland, heading for Oregon, and picks up Waylon, a Vietnam War veteran looking for shelter from a storm, and his Army buddy, Wayne, who rides a motorcycle. (G)

Awards/honors: BBYA; QP

Perrotta, Tom.

Election. **Putnam, 1998.** S A/YA

1

Winwood, New Jersey, is the setting for a political showdown: the student-body president election at Winwood High School. The candidate most likely to win is energetic overachiever Tracy Flick. It looks like Tracy will run unopposed, until popular history teacher and faculty advisor to the student government Jim McAllister encourages Paul Warren to run for office. Paul isn't as ambitious as Tracy, but he is popular, giving Tracy some competition. When her girlfriend Lisa leaves her to become Paul's girlfriend, Paul's anarchist sister Tammy decides to run against both Paul and Tracy. (L)

2

Peters, Julie Anne.

Between Mom and Jo. **Little, Brown, 2006.** J S

3

Since he was young Nick has been teased about having two moms, but the support he gets from his parents helps him to stand up for himself as he grows up, encountering typical angst about school and girls. Erin, his mom, and Jo, her partner, go through a lot, including alcoholism and cancer, but nothing affects Nick's life as much as their breakup. Erin refuses to let Nick and Jo see each other, a situation that addresses legal issues not often seen in books about children of divorce. (L)

4

Rapp, Adam.

Punkzilla. **Candlewick, 2009.** S

Jamie, fourteen and AWOL from military school, ekes out a living in Oregon by stealing iPods and giving the occasional hand job. He's also ditched his meds in favor of a trip to Memphis to visit his dying brother, Peter, who is gay and a playwright. The life of a street kid is shown in stark detail as Jamie finds trouble on one Greyhound bus after another. Though Peter never gets to see them, the end of the book reveals a series of letters Jamie wrote to Peter. (G)

5

Ripslinger, Jon.

How I Fell in Love and Learned to Shoot Free Throws. **Roaring Brook, 2003.** J S

6

Danny falls hard for Angel, aka Stone Angel, the new girl in town, who keeps a lot of secrets. Rumor has it that Angel is a lesbian, but as Danny gets to know her through her superior basketball skills, he finds out that it is actually her mother who is a lesbian. Danny and Angel are brought together by the fact that they each share a shameful secret. Danny's mother left his father for an ex and was killed in a motorcycle accident. The male point of view and sports details make this appealing for both boys and girls. (L)

7

Shimko, Annie.

Letters in the Attic. **Academy Chicago Publishers, 2002.** J S

In the worst twenty-four hours of Lizzy McMann's life, her father Manny announces that he's leaving her mother for the hat check girl at their hotel and that Lizzy and her mother must immediately vacate the hotel, which is their home. Her mother moves Lizzy from Arizona to New York, where Lizzy befriends Eva Singer. Lizzy quickly falls for Eva, but Eva does not reciprocate Lizzy's feelings, leaving Lizzy confused. Lizzy has more important things to worry about, though: Her mother might break up with Lizzy's teacher, whom she's been dating, to go back to Manny. (L)

Sones, Sonya.

🌲 *One of Those Hideous Books Where the Mother Dies.* **Simon & Schuster, 2004.** Ⓜ Ⓙ Ⓢ

High school junior Ruby knows two things about her father, Whip Logan: He's an award-winning actor and a sleaze. He left Ruby and her mother when Ruby was a baby to pursue a career in Hollywood. When Ruby's mother dies, Ruby is shipped out to LA. She's determined not to get along with her father, but finds she gets along well with his assistant, Max. Over time Ruby and her father begin to see eye to eye, and in the end Whip trusts Ruby enough to tell her that he is gay, and Max is more than just his assistant. (G)

Awards/honors: BBYA

Springer, Nancy.

Looking for Jamie Bridger. **Dial, 1995.** Ⓙ

At fourteen, Jamie has never known her parents; she was raised by her submissive grandmother and domineering grandfather, both of whom swore they never had children. When Jamie confronts her grandfather about her family history, he has a heart attack and dies. She takes matters into her own hands and discovers, after traveling to New York City, that her parents are actually her grandparents. A male Jamie Bridger whose picture she sees in an old yearbook is not her father but her brother, whom her parents disowned after learning he was gay. (G)

Trueman, Terry.

7 Days at the Hot Corner. **Harper, 2007.** Ⓙ Ⓢ

Baseball is everything to eighteen-year-old Scott, who spends the seven most nerve-racking days of his life waiting for the results of an AIDS test. After his best friend Travis tells Scott he's gay, Scott remembers a time when Travis bled on him and decides to get tested. In those seven days, an anonymous interview with a gay student runs in the school newspaper, and Scott's relationship with Travis is strained, even more so because Travis's parents threw him out of the house when he came out, and he now lives with Scott's family. (G)

Wilson, Martin.

What They Always Tell Us. **Delacorte, 2008.** Ⓢ

Alternating points of view focus on two brothers. On the surface, James is the more functional of the two. He is popular, plays tennis, and is anxiously awaiting his acceptance letter to Duke University. Alex drank Pine-Sol at a party and is secretly dating Nathen, one of James's friends. Alex knows that he has to keep his sexuality a secret, but Nathen turns out to have some positive influence on Alex's self-destructive behaviors. A mutual relationship with a neighbor boy brings James and Alex closer together. (G)

Winthrow, Sarah.

Box Girl. **Groundwood, 2001.** **M**

After Gwen's father began a relationship with Leon, her mother left for Europe. Five years later, Gwen's mother doesn't know a thing about Gwen and communicates via postcards. Gwen's ex-best friend reacted poorly to Gwen's telling her about her gay father, and since then she has decided that she'd rather be alone than have friends. She rejects friendly advances from the new girl, Clara, but when Clara reveals that she has some issues of her own, the two begin an honest friendship. (G)

Woodson, Jacqueline.

🌹 *After Tupac and D Foster.* **Putnam, 2008.** **M** **J**

An unnamed narrator and her best friend, Neeka, welcome the mysterious and fascinating D Foster into their group of friends. D tells Neeka and the narrator that she is a roamer, and that she came to their neighborhood in Queens because she liked the way it looked. The girls bond over their love of Tupac Shakur's music and are all equally devastated by news of his death. In a secondary plotline, Neeka's family is strained by her gay brother's incarceration for a hate crime he didn't commit. (G)

Awards/honors: Newbery Honor winner

🌹 *From the Notebooks of Melanin Sun.* **Scholastic, 1995.** **J** **S**

Melanin, who expresses many of his thoughts in notebooks rather than speaking them aloud, has never known his father but has a close relationship with his mother, a law student. His mother informs him she's a lesbian and introduces him to her girlfriend, a white lawyer named Kristin. Now Melanin has two identity issues to deal with: his mother's homosexuality and her interracial relationship. He works through his anger and confusion in his notebooks. When his friends find out about his mother, one abandons him, but another remains loyal. (L)

Awards/honors: Coretta Scott King Author Honor

🌹 *The House You Pass on the Way.* **Putnam, 2003.** **M** **J**

Isolation and desire are key themes of Staggerlee Canan. Because her mother is white, Staggerlee is an outcast in her mostly African American community. She also keeps the secret of the kiss she shared with another girl in sixth grade. When her cousin Trout comes to visit during the summer Staggerlee turns fourteen, she believes she's found someone she can confide her sexual feelings to. Trout and Staggerlee bond over the many ways they feel different from their peers. Although they grow apart in the end, what each girl takes from the relationship is important to her personal development. (L)

Awards/honors: BBYA

Yates, Bart.

🏆 *Leave Myself Behind.* **Kensington Publishing, 2003.** **A/YA**

Chicago native Noah York is critical of just about everything and wastes no time telling the world how he feels. His mother, a poet, accepts a teaching job in a small New Hampshire town after Noah's father dies. Although their relationship is mostly solid at first, they find Mason jars in the walls of their house containing letters and journal entries that eventually drive them apart. Noah deals with his sexuality at the same time he deals with the death of his father, and his voice is at once cynical and funny. Noah is a teen many can identify with. (G)

Awards/honors: Alex Award winner

Teen Romance

Teens love to read about love, regardless of their sexuality. These books cover both gay and straight romances; GLBTQ people play some kind of role in all of them, whether they are friends, parents, or romantic partners. These are teen, not adult, romances. Few of these characters have ever thought about any kind of long-term relationship or a happily-ever-after. Instead, teens might experiment, switch partners, or make discoveries about who they are through their relationships. GLBTQ characters may be in the forefront or on the sidelines in these books. Teens who enjoy reading stories about romance may also enjoy titles in the "First Love" section of chapter 1.

Barnes, Derrick.

🏆 *The Making of Dr. Truelove.* **Simon Pulse, 2006.** **S**

After a disastrous attempt at making love to his girlfriend Roxy, Diego feels like a failure in terms of romance. While Diego mourns his breakup, his best friend J-Live concocts a plan that will put Diego on the map with Casanova. Diego will take on the identity of Dr. Dexter Truelove, a hip sex advice columnist with all the right answers. After he establishes himself as wise in the ways of love, Diego plans to reveal his identity to Roxy. One of Diego's influences is his older, kind, confident sister Kris, an out lesbian with a popular syndicated radio show. (L)

Awards/honors: PPYA

Keywords: humor

Boock, Paula.

🏆 *Dare, Truth, or Promise.* **Houghton Mifflin, 1999.** **S**

Dual viewpoints are used in this story of a romance between two girls from very different backgrounds. Louie's parents are conservative, wealthy, and educated, and fiery Willa, still hurting from her first failed lesbian relationship, lives above a pub. The two meet while working at a local burger joint, and their connection is instantaneous. Their relationship faces many challenges, including a psychiatrist who tells Louie that her homosexuality is nothing more than a phase, but their love for each other helps them pull through. Familial support (from Willa's mother), or lack thereof (from Louie's), is an important theme. (L)

Awards/honors: Lambda Literary Award finalist; New Zealand Post Children's Book of the Year

Burnham, Niki.

Royally Jacked. Simon & Schuster, 2003. **M J**

Valerie's mom announces that she has fallen in love with another woman and is leaving Valerie's dad to move in with her. Given the option of living with her mom and her mom's vegan girlfriend, whom she's not quite ready to accept, or following her dad as he takes a job with the royal family of the country of Schwerinborg, she packs her bags. Never mind that she doesn't know anyone or speak the language. Things start to look up for Valerie when she meets the cute prince Georg and begins a romance. (L)

Keywords: humor

Hartinger, Brent.

🏵 *Order of the Poison Oak.* HarperTempest, 2005. **J S**

In the sequel to *Geography Club* (see chapter 1, "GLBTQ Identity") , sixteen-year-old Russel takes a summer job as a counselor at a summer camp. His first group of campers are survivors, ten-year-olds who have recovered physically from severe burns. Teenage hormones plus a close-knit environment result in love triangles and romance galore, but Russel has to deal with something a lot more challenging than his love life: ten-year-olds. After some unsuccessful attempts at discipline, Russel gains their respect by telling them a Native American folktale that parallels the plight of burn victims and homosexual people. When "his" kids are taunted for being burn victims and Russel says nothing, he loses everything he built with them and must start again, a metaphor for the damaging power of silence. (G, B)

Awards/honors: YALSA Teens Top Ten nominee

Johnson, Maureen.

The Bermudez Triangle. Razorbill, 2004. **M J S**

Mel, Avery, and Nina are best friends from upstate New York. The summer before their senior year, Nina attends a leadership workshop at Stanford University. While she is away, Mel and Avery work as waitresses at the same restaurant. Mel and Avery also begin a romantic relationship in Nina's absence. When Nina returns she has to sort out her feelings about their relationship. Ultimately, Avery decides to break up with Mel, date boys, and pursue a career as a musician, but Mel sees their relationship as confirmation of her sexuality. (B, L)

Jones, Carrie.

Tips on Having a Gay (ex) Boyfriend. Flux, 2007. **J S**

High school senior Belle believes that her relationship with Dylan is just about perfect, even heading for marriage, until Dylan tells her he's gay. Belle knows that Dylan's confession will make his life difficult in their rural Maine town, but she never anticipated that the same people who are prejudiced against Dylan could turn on her as well. Luckily, in the midst of the teasing and taunting she not only keeps a loyal friend, Emily, but discovers a new crush. The question lingers, though: What if all her boyfriends and crushes turn out to be gay? (G)

Love and Other Uses for Duct Tape. (Sequel). Flux, 2008. **S**

A few months after the end of the events of *Tips on Having a Gay Ex-Boyfriend*, everything seems to be going well for Belle. She, her best friend, and her mom are all in stable relationships, though she wishes her boyfriend was willing to go all the way. The all-around happiness begins to fade when Em shares a secret with Belle and keeping it takes a toll on both of them. In addition, Belle begins having seizures with no apparent trigger.

Klein, Norma.

My Life as a Body. Knopf, 1987. **S**

Augie, reserved and highly intelligent, is convinced that she'll never find romance, much less have sex. It seems to her that everyone in her high school is sexually experienced or at least sexually aware, including her lesbian best friend, Claudia. Sam was popular, with a hot girlfriend, until a car accident left him brain-damaged and in a wheelchair. Augie signs on to be Sam's tutor, and as Sam's mind returns to where it was before his car accident, he and Augie become sexually involved. They date during their senior year but part ways when they go off to college. (L)

Kluger, Steve.

Almost Like Being in Love. Perennial, 2004. **A/YA**

Opposites attract in this novel in letters, news articles, etc. Craig McKenna, football and baseball jock, and Travis Puckett, who's obsessed with Broadway musicals, fall in love in high school but lose touch when Travis heads to USC and Craig to Harvard. Twenty years after they leave high school, Travis is a history professor with a bad track record in love, and Craig is a humanitarian lawyer about to marry his boyfriend. Though they are both relatively happy, they've never forgotten each other, and Travis decides that he wants to be a part of Craig's life again. (G)

Keywords: alternative format

Levithan, David.

🏆 *Boy Meets Boy.* Knopf, 2003. **J S**

In a gay utopia better known as New Jersey, Paul falls in love with Noah. It's a classic story: Boy meets boy, boy falls in love with boy, boy royally screws up relationship with boy, boy gets boy back, but not without some serious work. Paul and Noah exist in a joyous place where the Homecoming Queen is also the captain of the football team and the straight kids get fashion tips from the gay kids. There is still some opposition to homosexuality from Paul's best friend's parents, but the relationships among the students are loyal and caring. (G, L, B, T)

Awards/honors: BBYA; BCCB Blue Ribbon Award; PPYA

Levithan, David, and Rachel Cohn.

Naomi and Ely's No Kiss List. Knopf, 2007. **S**

Naomi and Ely's relationship is more than just a friendship; it's an institution. They've created a No-Kiss List, a list of people who are off limits for either Naomi or Ely (as far as kissing is concerned), which is supposed to alleviate jealousies in their friendship. All is mostly well with the No-Kiss List, except for two things. First, Naomi is in love with Ely, something much more than platonic, and she pretends to be okay with the fact that he's gay. Second, Ely violates one of the primary rules of any friendship when he kisses Naomi's boyfriend. (G)

♣ *Nick and Norah's Infinite Playlist.* Knopf, 2006. **S**

Nick is the straight bass player of a queercore high school punk band. Norah is in the audience at one of Nick's shows. When Nick sees his ex-girlfriend in the audience, he turns to Norah and asks if she will be his girlfriend for five minutes. In one night, Nick and Norah get together, break up, and get back together again. Nick and Norah's relationship is a highly appealing duet, told in alternating voices with a lot of stream-of-consciousness writing. (G)

Awards/honors: BBYA; PPYA

Keywords: alternate format

Maclean, Judy.

Rosemary and Juliet. Harrington Park Press, 2004. **J** **S**

Shakespeare gets a modern update. Romey is the only out lesbian at her high school and has support at home from her ex-hippie, pro-choice mother. Romey is grateful for her two close friends, straight Amina and gay Elliot, but she worries about ever finding romance. Julie, a gifted singer with the church choir, is homeschooled by her devout Christian father, who is head of the Divido Bible Church. Julie feels conflicted about her passion for Romey. How could a Christian girl be a lesbian? Maclean uses ethereal, descriptive language that may appeal to romance fans. (G, L)

Manning, Sara.

Pretty Things. Dutton, 2005. **S**

North Londoner Brie loves Charlie, who loves Walker, who loves Daisy. Their four-way love parallels a production of *The Taming of the Shrew* in which they are all participating. Walker is straight and leading gay Charlie on, and Daisy, a lesbian, enjoys being with Walker as much as she does being with her girlfriend. To Charlie, who sadly admits that he usually only fancies straight guys, his sexual orientation is not the be-all and end-all of his identity, and he offers to have sex with Brie. Sex, love, and relationships are explored as separate, yet intertwined, things. (G, L, B)

Mastbaum, Brian.

🏵 *Clay's Way*. **Alyson Books, 2004.** **S**

Sam's nerdy friends, mundane middle-class parents, stereotypically Hawaiian neighbors, and inability to do all the skateboard tricks he wants to frustrate him. He's into dying his hair punk colors and writing bad haikus. When he meets Clay, Sam's feelings move quickly from interest to crush to obsession. He gives up his best friend for Clay and enters into some destructive behaviors. Sam has to wonder, though, if Clay is really deserving of Sam's intense, even roller coaster-like feelings. Does he really love Clay, or does Clay's nonconformity, even defiance, simply represent what Sam wants to be? Strong language abounds. (G)

Awards/honors: Lambda Literary Award winner

Sanchez, Alex.

🏵 *Rainbow Boys*. **Simon & Schuster, 2001.** **S**

Nelson, brash and fashionable, is out to the world. His best friend Kyle, a smart, somewhat shy jock, is gay, but no one knows except Nelson. Popular basketball star Jason, as far as he's ever known, is straight, and he even has a girlfriend. The book alternates among Jason's, Kyle's, and Nelson's points of view as they struggle with dating, school, family, and in Jason's case, coming to terms with his sexuality. A romance blossoms between Jason and Kyle even as Nelson, who makes an unsafe attempt to meet a boyfriend online, confesses his crush on Kyle. This book crosses into the "life issues" category as well, with Jason's discovery of his sexuality. (G, B, Q)

Awards/honors: BBYA

Shaw, Tucker.

The Hookup Artist. **HarperCollins, 2006.** **J** **S**

Lucas is the Dolly Levi of his high school, a talented matchmaker who hasn't been lucky in love. Everyone at his school wants to make use of his expertise in matchmaking, particularly his best friend Cate, who is on the rebound from being recently dumped and is looking for the next Mr. Right, or at least Mr. Right Now. Lucas matches Cate with the hot new kid, Derek. Cate is dubious about Lucas's intentions for her relationship with Derek, especially because Lucas can't seem to keep his eyes off Derek. This is a new twist on an old story, told with humor and realistic dialogue. (G)

Keywords: humor

Stoehr, Shelley.

Tomorrow Wendy. **Bantam Dell, 1998.** **S**

On the surface, high school senior Cary is fearless, with a style all her own and a willingness to experiment with drugs. Inside, however, she's not as sassy as she seems. She's sleeping with Danny, but despite her open disdain of the out lesbians at school, she's really crushing on Danny's sister, Wendy, who has eyes only for a drug addict with tattoos. Also on the scene is Raven, a comfortable, out lesbian whose mother fully supports her. Raven falls in love with Cary, while trying to help Cary sort out her Wendy dilemma. (L)

Von Ziegesar, Cecily.

Gossip Girl series.

This series follows a crowd of the richest, naughtiest teens in Manhattan through private school, parties, romances, road trips, college applications and acceptances, and family changes. High school juniors Blair, Nathan, Serena, Daniel, and Vanessa and freshman Jenny hook up, break up, and make up. The series narrator, the catty, anonymous Gossip Girl, shares all the dirty details of Manhattan's finest with readers of her Web site. In one story line, Blair's father leaves her mother for another man and lives with his partner in Paris. Blair maintains a relationship with her father that is about as functional as any other parent–child relationship in the series. (G)

Gossip Girl. Little, Brown, 2002. **S**

You Know You Love Me. Little, Brown, 2002. **S**

All I Want Is Everything. Little, Brown, 2003. **S**

Because I'm Worth It. Little, Brown, 2004. **S**

I Like It Like That. Little, Brown, 2004. **S**

You're the One That I Want. Little, Brown, 2004. **S**

Nobody Does It Better. Little, Brown, 2005. **S**

Nothing Can Keep Us Together. Little, Brown, 2005. **S**

Would I Lie to You? Little, Brown, 2006. **S**

Only in Your Dreams. Little, Brown, 2006. **S**

Don't You Forget About Me. Little, Brown, 2007. **S**

Wersba, Barbara.

Just Be Gorgeous. HarperCollins, 1988. **J S**

Heidi can't help but fall for Jeffrey. All her life, Heidi's mom has nagged her about her looks, and Jeffrey, a former foster child living on the streets, is the one person in her life who accepts her as is and doesn't think she needs to improve the way she looks. Jeffrey's sunny outlook helps Heidi gain some insight about her needs and wants. In the end Heidi realizes that Jeffrey can never love her romantically, and he leaves town with a gay couple who offer him a new life. (G)

Wittlinger, Ellen.

🏵 *Hard Love.* Simon & Schuster, 1999. **J S**

Before MySpace, there were zines. John Galardi, zine enthusiast, is a fan of Marisol Guzman's zine, *Escape Velocity*, and is determined to meet her. John has shut off most of his emotions, separating himself from his emotionally and physically distant parents. Until he falls for Marisol he's convinced he has no feelings left at all, and he is thrilled when Marisol's feelings for him seem positive. Unfortunately for John, Marisol is a lesbian and not entirely sure how she can let him down without destroying their friendship. (L, Q)

Awards/honors: BBYA; Lambda Literary Award; Printz Honor

Love and Lies: Marisol's Story. **(Sequel). Simon & Schuster, 2008.** 🅂

Instead of going to Stanford right after high school, Marisol decides to stay home for a year and write a novel. She takes a waitressing job and enrolls in a community college writing course. The course instructor, Olivia, is beautiful and significantly older than Marisol. During the course, Marisol starts to repair her damaged friendship with Gio and falls hard for Olivia. Marisol's friends can see that her relationship with Olivia is nothing but damaging, but Marisol has to make her own mistakes and learn about love the hard way. (G, L)

Heart on My Sleeve. **Simon & Schuster, 2004.** 🅹 🅂

Chloe, from Massachusetts, and Julian, from Florida, meet on a college visit and keep in touch via e-mails, letters, and instant messaging for months afterward. Their relationship causes problems for both of them offline, even engendering Chloe's breakup with her boyfriend. When they get the chance to meet again in person, their meeting is not the happy reunion either of them had planned. Chloe's sister coming out as a lesbian is one of a few subplots, all of which are tied together around the theme of identity, self-knowledge, and the question of how well you can know another person when your relationship isn't face to face. (L)

Woodson, Jacqueline.

🌳 *If You Come Softly.* **Putnam, 1998.** 🅼 🅹

Family issues and bigotry surround fifteen-year-old Miah, one of the few African American students at his exclusive New York City private school, and his classmate Ellie, a white transfer student. Ellie's relationship with her mother, who has twice abandoned the family, is strained. Miah's parents are divorced, and he splits his time between their apartments. Drawn together by their similar family problems, Miah and Ellie fall in love. Their relationship, though caring, is fraught with difficulties because of racism on the part of other people, and their strong love cannot see them through to a completely happy ending. (L)

Awards/honors: BBYA

Collections and Anthologies

The following short story collections address issues of friendship, family, or romance—or combinations of all three.

Appelt, Kathi.

🌳 *Kissing Tennessee and Other Stories from the Stardust Dance.* **Harcourt, 2000.** 🅼 🅹

The Stardust Dance, the last dance before eighth-grade graduation, is just hours away. Eight short stories from different points of view each focus on eight students at Dogwood Junior High as they each get ready for the dance. Peggy Lee and Tennessee shared a kiss in first grade and are about to share their second. Becca's boyfriend rapes her, and she spends much of the dance alone. The GLBTQ content comes from Cub's story, in which he faces his attraction to boys even though he tries to avoid what he calls "The Question." (G)

Awards/honors: BBYA; QP

Cart, Michael, ed.

Necessary Noise: Stories About Our Families as They Really Are. **HarperCollins, Joanna Cotler Books, 2003.** **M** **J** **S**

Ten stories from well-known, critically acclaimed authors (including Sonya Sones, Joan Bauer, and Walter Dean Myers) reflect all different kinds of families, including shared communities, single-parent, and same-sex partnerships. Of particular interest to GLBTQ readers is Rita Williams-Garcia's "A Woman's Touch," told from the point of view of a boy with two mothers, Moms and Momo. Even though Jason knows he and his mother and brother are better off being away from his physically abusive father, he still wonders who will teach him what he needs to know about manhood. (L)

Keywords: short stories

Block, Francesca Lia.

🎗 *Girl Goddess #9.* **HarperCollins, 1996.** **S**

Nine short stories center around girls, the people they love, and the ups and downs of adolescence. The two stories of highest interest to GLBTQ teen readers are "Dragons in Manhattan," in which a girl travels from New York to California in search of her father, only to learn that her father is transgender and is actually one of her two mothers, and "Winnie and Cubby," in which a boy comes out to his girlfriend. Block's lyrical writing and majestic descriptions appeal to many fantasy readers. (G, L, T)

Awards/honors: BBYA

Crutcher, Chris.

🎗 *Athletic Shorts.* **Greenwillow, 1991.** **J** **S**

Characters from Crutcher's popular titles *Stotan!* (HarperTeen, 1986) and *Running Loose* (HarperTeen, 1983) join new, original characters in this collection of six short stories. Of particular interest to GLBT readers are "A Brief Moment in the Life of Angus Bethune," about a boy with four parents, and "In the Time I Get," in which Louie Banks from *Running Loose* meets a young man with AIDS. (G)

Awards/honors: QP

Wallace, Rich.

Losing Is Not an Option: Stories. **Knopf, 2003.** **J** **S**

This collection consists of nine interrelated stories set in Wallace's familiar territory of Sturbridge, Pennsylvania, and centered on Ron, a runner and poet. The stories follow Ron from sixth grade through twelfth, chronicling important events with his family, friends, and attempts at love. The story of particular interest to GLBT readers is "Letters That Would Soar a Thousand

Feet High," in which Ron is invited by a runner from a neighboring town to a party whose attendees are mostly gay. Despite his lack of style around girls, he handles the uncomfortable party situation with grace. (G)

Chapter 3

Issues

As in many young adult novels, the focus in these books is on issues such as abuse and dysfunctional families. However, in these books the issues are specifically tied to sexual identity. Although many of these books could also fit in chapter 2, "Contemporary Realistic Fiction," with books in which a character's sexuality is only one complicated aspect of his or her multidimensional life, here issues related to the character's sexuality become the driving force behind the plot. The primary plotline or point of conflict of these books often follows events related to a character's first realization of his or her sexuality or a first same-sex romance; the mood of these books is generally darker.

Think twice before suggesting these titles to a GLBTQ teen who is just starting to question his or her sexuality, because they may lead teens to conclude that their behavior will somehow be punished. The feelings of the main characters in these novels are valid and real, and books that discuss the effects of abuse on a person's sexuality belong in the library collection. When doing readers' advisory in this GLBTQ subgenre, however, be sure to conduct a thorough interview before making recommendations. The content and mood of a book and the main character's feelings about his or her sexuality are key elements in matching the right book to the reader.

Even though the exploration of one's sexual identity can be stressful and serious, not all the books in this section are solemn and/or depressing. As in much teen literature, there are hopeful if not happy endings for many otherwise serious books. The characters in these books often face seemingly insurmountable challenges and undergo tremendous struggles, not only with themselves but with their family and friends, especially where coming out is concerned. Although GLBTQ teens may be welcomed and accepted at the library, they are not always welcome at school or by their families. These "issue" books represent reactions from across the spectrum. They also show that sometimes the person the main character believes will have the most difficult time accepting his or her coming out is the most supportive.

Because no one can exist in a social vacuum, and books need comparison points, technically the books in this section can all be considered "contemporary life." They are included here because of the theme of struggle surrounding sexual identity.

Four books in this subgenre are worth mentioning separately: *Target* by Kathleen Jeffrie Johnson, *When Jeff Comes Home* by Catherine Atkins, *Boy O'Boy* by Brian Doyle (see under "Abuse" in this chapter), and *33 Snowfish* by Adam Rapp. Although these are all quality works of literature by talented authors, they may not be the best books to give a GLBTQ teen who is just starting to question his or her sexuality, because the issues surrounding the main characters' sexualities are engendered by violence and/or abuse at the hands of people they cannot control, not by self-discovery or the naturally developing feelings of adolescent crushes. The feelings of the main characters in these novels are valid and real, and books that discuss the aftereffects of abuse on a person's sexuality do belong in the library collection. A reader who is interested in the effects of abuse on sexuality (or abuse, period) will probably be more interested in these four books, but readers who simply wish to learn more about their sexual feelings may not be the best match for them.

This chapter is divided into four sections: "Teen Angst," "Outcasts and Outsiders: Discrimination, Homophobia, and Bullying," "Abuse," and "Dysfunctional Families." Some of the titles in this chapter could be considered historical fiction, but their emphasis is more on the theme rather than the setting. Therefore they are placed here and have the keywords "historical setting" and an era.

Teen Angst

No one understands what it's like to be me! Those words, or variations on them, are quite familiar to all of us. If we didn't utter them ourselves, we know teens who do. It's normal for every teen to go through questions of identity, especially as identity is connected to sexuality and dating. For some teens, confidence in their sexual orientation is not an issue. Girls are sure they want to date boys, and boys are sure they want to date girls; their concern is *which* boy or girl to date. For others, this question is tied to, "Is she like I am?" or "Am I doomed if I'm gay and she's not and she finds out?" That's where these books come in. This section describes titles in which sexual orientation and identity somehow result in negative feelings and reactions.

Alphin, Elaine Marie.

Simon Says. Harcourt, 2002. **S**
> Charles Weston has the ability to convey amazing emotion and candid truth in his paintings, which makes people fear him. The high school junior transfers to Whitman, an arts boarding school, and meets Graeme, a writer whom he admires. Charles is on a mission to have people like him for who he is, someone more than just a gifted painter. He believes that Graeme does like him, but he realizes that Graeme, like the characters in his YA novel, is playing games, saying and doing what he thinks everyone else wants him to say and do. Then Graeme embarks on a deadly endeavor. (G)

Atkins, Catherine.

Alt Ed. Putnam, 2003. **J** **S**
> Lonely, overweight Susan, a high school sophomore who is teased at school, decides to take revenge on Kale, one of her tormentors, by teaming up with openly gay Brendan Slater and defacing Kale's truck. When she and Brendan are caught, the only thing that will save them from expulsion is their attendance at an after-school discussion group. They are joined by four fellow students in trouble,

including Kale himself. At first Susan is terrified to speak, but the group, whose only rule is that all discussions remain confidential, inspires Susan to take charge of her life and work on improving her friendship with Brendan. (G)

Cameron, Peter.

Someday This Pain Will Be Useful to You. **Farrar, Straus & Giroux, 2007.** **S**

To James Sveck, a modern "Holden Caulfield," most people are phonies. Rather than confront people, eighteen-year-old James withdraws into a silent existence. His divorced parents, who don't understand him, send him to talk to a psychologist. James does discuss his homosexuality with Dr. Adler, but his sexuality is only a small component of his larger story and the issues that lead to his self-imposed solitude. James's need to be separated from others leads him to search for a home in the Midwest, away from the noise and people of Manhattan and the stresses of Brown University, where he is headed in the fall. (G)

Cooper, Melrose.

Life Magic. **Holt, 1996.** **M**

Sixth-grader Crystal often feels like a failure. Her best friend Shawna is an accomplished dancer, and her older sister Janelle is a published author; Crystal still struggles with reading and needs reading tutoring several times a week. When her uncle Joe moves from California to Buffalo, Crystal feels that she's found someone who understands her. Unfortunately Joe grows weaker and sick over time and tells her that he is dying of AIDS. As Crystal grieves, an encounter with the class bully shows her that she is not the only one who has lost family members to the disease. (G)

Fullerton, Alma.

In the Garage. **Red Deer Press, 2006.** **J** **S**

Social acceptance is Barbara Jean (B.J.)'s raison d'être. But she has a port wine stain (a birthmark) on her face, is overweight, and is often targeted for teasing by her classmates. The one person who is loyal to her and nonjudgmental is Alex. Then David joins Alex's garage band and Alex pays a lot more attention to David than he does to B.J. Because of her need for acceptance, B.J. betrays Alex to two of the most popular girls in school, Victoria and Rachel, who act like B.J.'s best friends, by stealing Alex's journal, in which he confesses his feelings about David. (G)

Hrdlitschka, Shelley.

❦ *Dancing Naked.* **Orca, 2001.** **S**

Stable, churchgoing Kia is in a terrifying situation: She's pregnant and not in a position to take care of a baby. Her boyfriend urges her to abort, but Kia doesn't believe that abortion is the right decision for her. The sixteen-year-old chronicles the pregnancy through the course of the book and exchanges e-mails with Justin, a Unitarian youth counselor. She wants them to be together as a couple and raise the baby, but Justin is gay, and eventually Kia realizes their relationship can't be anything but platonic. When the baby is born, Kia is faced with a tough decision. (G)

Awards/honors: PPYA; QP

Huser, Glen.

Stitches. **Groundwood Books, 2003.** **M** **J**

Puppets and puppeteering are Travis's escape from his tumultuous life. He lives with his aunt and uncle in a trailer while his mother works as a lounge singer. His best friend Chantelle, who walks with a limp, rescued him from name-calling bullies in fifth grade, but as junior high progresses the bullies' taunts escalate to violence. Travis is mired in hopelessness, but he also has a life with beauty and people who care about him. He stays true to what he likes, even though his pursuit of a "feminine" art means brings torment with it. (G, Q)

Hyde, Catherine Ryan.

Becoming Chloe. **Knopf, 2006.** **S**

When Jordan came out to his parents, his homophobic father nearly killed him. He ekes out a living by hustling on the streets of New York. While living in an abandoned building, he rescues an eighteen-year-old girl from a gang rape. Although her full backstory is never revealed, Jordan gleans that her existence has been brutal and ugly. To find beauty, Jordan and the girl he names Chloe take a cross-country trek, hitchhiking and bicycling, relying on the kindness of strangers. In traveling, Jordan and Chloe find the beauty they've been searching for. (G)

Saenz, Benjamin Alire.

🎗 *Sammy and Juliana in Hollywood*. **Cinco Puntos Press, 2004.** **J** **S**

Sammy's Hollywood, a barrio in Las Cruces, New Mexico, is about as far from the LA Hollywood as one can get. The Vietnam War is raging, and high school senior Sammy, called "The Librarian" by his friends because of his love for books and knowledge, is uncertain where the future will take him. His girlfriend Juliana and her family are brutally murdered by her father, and at school there are protests against a dress code and teachers who are unsympathetic to the students' complex feelings. In one plotline, gay neighbors leave the barrio so they can continue to live together. (G)

Awards/honors: BBYA

Keywords: 1960s; historical setting

Outcasts and Outsiders: Discrimination, Homophobia, and Bullying

"That's so gay!" "We really would prefer it if you didn't flaunt your lifestyle at this school." "Girls take sewing and boys take wood shop." From bullying to discipline to a life plan determined by gender, teens get messages about what is and what is not acceptable in their schools and homes as a proper way to express themselves. It's easy to change clothing, but a teen who does not fit into standard gender roles for any reason may be the subject of bullying and harassment, not just from peers but also parents, school administrators, and other adults they are supposed to be able to trust. Though they may be silenced in their daily lives, their stories and inner thoughts can come alive in books.

The stories in this section have one common thread: Bullying is related to the main character's sexual orientation. Not every story is told by the bullied person; in a few, the bullied teen barely makes an appearance. These stories depend on someone else to get the message out about the harassment GLBTQ students face in their daily lives.

Brande, Robin.

Evolution, Me, and Other Freaks of Nature. **Knopf, 2007.** **M** **J** **S**
From the beginning of this book, the reader knows that Mena is a social outcast, ignored and tormented by the members of her church youth group, but the motivation behind her high school classmates' behavior is not clear. In science class, she is partnered with cute Casey, who gives her the strength to stand up to her former friends when the class studies evolution. As the book progresses, the reader learns that Mena was the sole person from the group to apologize to a gay classmate who attempted suicide after being harassed by church members. (G)

Gantos, Jack.

Desire Lines. **Farrar, Straus & Giroux, 1997.** **S**
Walker, a loner at his high school, resists associating with the fundamentalist Christians who make no bones about their dislike of homosexuals. Because of his reticence to join in taunting other homosexual teens, Walker, who is not gay, becomes the target of a witch hunt instigated by the local preacher. To escape persecution and maintain a macho image, Walker points a finger at a lesbian couple whom he has seen having sex at the golf course he frequents. When the girls' secret goes public, they take drastic measures. (L)

Garden, Nancy.

The Year They Burned the Books. **Farrar, Straus & Giroux, 1999.** **J** **S**
High school newspaper editor Jamie has a lot on her plate. A fundamentalist member of the school governing board leads a motion to ignore the school's sex-education curriculum and stage a book burning on Halloween. The faculty editor of the school paper, who supports a more liberal view, is forced into a leave of absence, and her replacement forbids Jamie to write any editorials that might be considered controversial. In the midst of this turmoil, Jamie is falling for Tessa, the artistic new girl from Boston. The focus on political issues means that characters' emotions don't get as much screen time, but there is much to discuss about discrimination and ethics. (L)

Keywords: censorship

Greene, Bette.

The Drowning of Stephan Jones. **Delacorte, 1991.** **S**

In a small Southern town, sixteen-year-old Carla lives with her mother, a liberal librarian. She wants more than anything to be a part of the in-crowd at school, which she achieves by dating popular Andy Harris. When a gay couple moves to town from Boston, homophobic Andy begins a virulent, then murderous campaign of harassment. Carla has to decide whether to risk her social status and Andy's love by standing up for the gay couple, Stephan and Frank. Carla is not a lesbian, nor are her friends or family members. The persecution of a gay couple that Carla witnesses is something many teens still see today and may factor into their daily lives. (G)

Hurwin, Davida Willis.

Freaks and Revelations. **Little, Brown, 2009.** **S**

This is a fictionalized account of the lives of Matthew Boger and Timothy Zaal, who now work as teachers at the Museum of Tolerance. The first narrator, Doug, is a seventeen-year-old neo-Nazi who loves punk rock. Jason, the second narrator, is thirteen and gay, living on the streets after being thrown out of his religious family. One night in 1980, Doug beats Jason in a hate crime. Years later, the two meet as part of a joint project at the Museum of Tolerance, and they recognize each other. (G)

Keywords: historical fiction

Mac, Carrie.

The Beckoners. **Orca, 2007.** **S**

Once again, fifteen-year-old Zoe has to move because of her mother's job, this time to the conservative town of Abbotsford, whose school is run by vicious Beck and her gang, the Beckoners. Beck takes an interest in Zoe and initiates her into the Beckoners against her will. Because of her fear of Beck, Zoe keeps quiet when she witnesses bullying and violence. She eventually begins to see that she cannot break away from Beck on her own and enlists the help of Leaf, her boyfriend; April, the Beckoners' constant victim; and a gay couple, Simon and Teo, to stop the Beckoners for good. (G)

Murrow, Liza Ketchum.

🏅 *Twelve Days in August.* **Holiday House, 1993.** **J** **S**

Todd is ready to start his junior year on a high note, playing varsity soccer and dating Kai. Then twins Alex and Rita move to town, and Alex impresses the soccer team with his athletic skill. Todd admires Alex's skill on the soccer field, but other teammates see Alex as a threat, and they suspect he's gay. Using homophobic name-calling and bullying, Todd's teammate Randy hopes that Alex will quit. Todd can't agree with Randy's actions and consequently questions his own feelings about Alex. Later, Todd's uncle reveals that he also is gay. (G)

Awards/honors: BBYA

Shyer, Marlene Fanta.

The Rainbow Kite. **Marshall Cavendish, 2002. M J**

Twelve-year-old Matthew narrates the story of his older brother Bennett's depressive downward spiral. After the death of their dog, Bennett loses interest in his activities and friends and is taunted by school bullies. Things start to look up for Bennett when he befriends their new neighbor, Jeremy. Together, Bennett and Jeremy build a rainbow kite, which they plan to fly over their eighth-grade graduation, but a gang commits a homophobic hate crime against Bennett. Matthew and Bennett's homophobic father changes his tune, and Bennett's spirits are lifted by a graduation present from a lesbian couple. (G, L)

Zalben, Jane Breskin.

Unfinished Dreams. **Simon & Schuster, 1996. M**

Sixth-grader Jason has aspirations of being a professional violinist, and his popular, understanding principal, Mr. Carr, is helping him to realize that dream. Mr. Carr has AIDS, and as his health declines, rumors about his homosexuality spread around the school. Jason must try to dodge the school bully as well as navigate through the homophobic comments his classmates hear at home and then repeat at school. Jason's first-person narrative brings his emotions close to the reader, and his hold on kindness helps him to grow throughout the book. (G)

Abuse

Abuse stories have always been and will always be popular with teen readers, and they need to be told. Abuse, whether it's physical, sexual, or emotional, happens every day. It happens among families and in dating relationships. It also raises a tough collection development question: If it's hard enough to rationalize collecting books with GLBTQ characters, how can adding *more* problems to these books make the decision to add them easier? Isn't it more important to have "happy" GLBTQ books, to make teens understand that they are accepted in the library? Wouldn't showing abusive relationships of any kind in GLBTQ books just prove that they'll be punished for engaging in a same-sex relationship?

The answer to all of these questions is, in short, no. Here's why: Abuse happens.

Is this an oversimplified answer? No. The fact is, no number of "happy" books on any library's shelf will prevent abuse from happening. What books about abusive relationships will do is show GLBTQ teens and their allies that an abusive relationship can happen to anyone, and if you're in one, you're not alone. Dating violence is a big concern for many teens. When Grammy-winning R&B singer Chris Brown confessed in 2009 to hitting his girlfriend, it became national news and a national debate. Books, especially books like *Rage* by Julie Anne Peters, show that love cannot necessarily conquer abuse in a violent relationship. Abusers in these books, whether they abuse physically, sexually, or emotionally, affect teens of many different backgrounds.

Books about abuse also show that teens in abusive relationships need understanding and a place to heal. Every book offers this in a different way, via friends, family, other caring adults, or supernatural creatures.

Atkins, Catherine.

🏵 *When Jeff Comes Home*. **Putnam, 1999.** 🇯 🇸

Almost three years after being abducted by a man named Ray, sixteen-year-old Jeff is returned to his family. Ray's sexual abuse makes Jeff question his own sexuality and his attachment to Ray. In the first part of the book, Jeff denies the effects of Ray's abuse, and the reader sees Jeff's family adjust to his return. When Ray is caught, around the midpoint of the book, Jeff's denial of Ray's wrongdoings begins to break down. Throughout Jeff's recovery, his relationship with his father, once close, becomes strained. (G)

Awards/honors: BBYA

Block, Francesca Lia.

🏵 *I Was a Teenage Fairy*. **HarperCollins, 1998.** 🇸

Eleven-year-old Barbie (like the doll) is pushed into modeling against her will by her mother, who is unsympathetic even when Barbie tells her she's been molested by a photographer. As a result of the molestation, Barbie sees a fairy, Mab. Mab is smart and witty, and she encourages Barbie to move beyond the many hurtful events in her life. At age sixteen, Barbie has a modeling career and a celebrity boyfriend, Todd. It turns out that Todd's gay roommate, Griffin, was molested by the same photographer who abused Barbie and can also see Mab. (G)

Awards/honors: Lambda Literary Awards; QP

Chambers, Aidan.

Dance on My Grave. **Harper, 1982.** 🇸

High-schoolers Hal and Barry share a whirlwind seven-week romance, and during this time Barry makes Hal promise that if one of them dies, the other must dance on his grave. Their relationship ends in a fight over a girl Barry has spent the night with, and in Barry's rush to get away from Hal, he crashes his motorcycle and dies. The book opens with a newspaper item about Hal (unnamed by the paper) being arrested for dancing on a friend's grave. Through Hal's memories and the notes of his court-appointed social worker, we learn about the unbalanced nature of the boys' relationship and Hal's need for love and human closeness. (G)

Doyle, Brian.

Boy O'Boy. **Groundwood, 2004.** 🇲 🇯

In 1945, Martin is a member of a summer boys' choir, where he can escape his parents' fighting and his profoundly disabled brother. The organist for the choir is Mr. George, who takes a particular, inappropriate interest in Martin. After drugging Martin, Mr. George sexually abuses him, which confuses Martin because Mr. George had given him money and Martin believed that he was a good man. When Martin discovers that Mr. George is also molesting his best friend Billy, the boys concoct a plan to take revenge on their abuser. (G)

Keywords: historical setting; World War II

Johnson, Kathleen Jeffrie.

Target. **Roaring Brook, 2003.** **S**

Grady, who is repeating eleventh grade at a new school, is harboring a secret: He survived being brutally raped by two men, and his parents have honored his request to transfer to a school where no one knows him. Since the rape, Grady has stopped eating and spends hours listening to bluegrass music, paralyzed by memories of the rape and what it means for his sexuality. At his new school, he makes new, loyal friends who accept him even when he tells them his secret. (G)

Awards/honors: BBYA

Knowles, Jo.

Lessons from a Dead Girl. **Candlewick, 2007.** **S**

Told in simple, spare language, this story opens when sixteen-year-old Lainey learns that her best friend from childhood, Leah, died in a car accident. Lainey's memory takes the reader from fifth grade through her junior year in high school, demonstrating that being Leah's friend meant popularity, but it also meant abuse. Leah and Lainey's relationship had a dark physical side to it as well, in which sex and sexuality were not necessarily the same thing. Truth, lies, and secrets tied Leah and Lainey together, and Leah had no qualms about bending all of them. (G, Q)

Oates, Joyce Carol.

Freaky Green Eyes. **HarperTempest, 2003.** **S**

After surviving a near date rape, fifteen-year-old Francesca, or Frankie, develops a new, darker personality that she calls Freaky Green Eyes. Underneath his charismatic public personality, Frankie's wealthy sportscaster father is abusive, and he is physically violent when things don't go the way he wants them to. Frankie's mother disappears with a gay male friend, disrupting the delicate family balance, and Frankie is angered by this. (G)

Sexy. **HarperTeen, 2005.** **S**

Since sixteen-year-old Darren Flynn filled out and grew into his looks, he's been attracting a lot attention from both girls and boys. Darren, whose life is not as privileged as that of many of his classmates, finds the attention both disquieting and exciting. When his English teacher, Mr. Tracy, flunks one of Darren's swimming teammates, the teammates retaliate by framing Mr. Tracy as a pedophile. Now Darren must decide if he will stand up for his teacher. Darren's sexuality remains a question throughout the course of the novel. (G, Q)

Peters, Julie Anne.

Rage: A Love Story. **Knopf, 2009.** **S**

Johanna is known for being reliable and dependable, steadfast even in times of turmoil. Her crush, Reeve, has a lot of anger and a very short fuse. When Johanna takes a gig tutoring Reeve's brother, the two girls begin a tumultuous relationship. Even though Reeve says she loves Johanna, she cannot contain her rage and abuses Johanna, striking her in anger. Johanna must then decide if her loyalty to and love for Reeve are worth more than her own physical safety. (L)

Rapp, Adam.

33 Snowfish. **Candlewick, 2003.** **S**

Three teens, one of whom only communicates with the reader through pictures, are on the run from the law for various reasons. Boobie has kidnapped his baby brother and intends to sell him. Curl, Boobie's fifteen-year-old girlfriend, is a prostitute. As Curl and Boobie drive they pick up preteen Custis, who is on the run from his "owner," a man who sexually abused him. On the road, their stories unfold. Rapp's trademark is his use of harsh but lyrical language and unforgiving looks at abusive, dire situations. (G)

Toten, Theresa.

The Game. **Red Deer Press, 2001.** **J** **S**

Dani Webster's suicide attempt lands her in Riverwood, a facility for troubled teens. Her fellow residents include her roommate Scratch, who never receives any visitors, and Kevin, who is mentally healthy. Kevin's religious parents committed him to Riverwood after he came out to them and resisted reprogramming. Through her group and individual therapy sessions, the truth behind Dani's suicide attempt becomes clear: Her father was abusive, setting abnormally high standards for perfection, and his behavior had adverse effects on the entire Webster family. (G)

Dysfunctional Families

Personal identity and sexuality isn't the only source of angst for GLBTQ teens. Their families and people closest to them can often be the cause of many of their problems and hurt them the most. Instead of supporting one another and working through tough times, the protagonists of these books find that their families antagonize them. Even if these teens don't deal directly with homophobia in their families, their family members might be too caught up in their own problems to help them. A dysfunctional family at home might cause a teen to run from his or her problems, which can make those problems even worse. One dysfunctional family can have a ripple effect on other characters in the book, too, especially if it's the family of a close friend of the protagonist.

Brooks, Martha.

✤ *Mistik Lake*. **Groundwood, 2007.** **J** **S**

Odella is dealing with a lot of family trauma. Her parents divorced after her mother ran off to Iceland with a younger man. Gloria, Odella's great-aunt, hides her lesbianism from everyone in their small town. The novel revolves around the damaging power of secrets. Sally, Odella's mother, runs away partly to escape the guilt she feels over being the sole survivor of a car accident. Odella and her sisters work to conceal their mother's drinking. When Sally dies in an accident, the family must come together to work through their grief. Told from multiple viewpoints. (L)

Awards/honors: BBYA

Burchill, Julie.

Sugar Rush. **HarperTeen, 2005.** [S]

Fifteen-year-old Kim's life in Brighton, England, is upset when her mother leaves her father for a twenty-eight-year-old man and moves to the Caribbean. Her father falls on rough financial times, and Kim must transfer from exclusive Preston High to Riverdene, a high school she has heard horror stories about. At Riverdene isefriended by Maria, aka Sugar, who invites her to become a part of the popular clique of bad girls. Kim finds herself falling for Maria, but Maria's manipulative behavior is dangerous. Ultimately Maria betrays Kim, but Kim is able to move forward with her life. (L)

Donovan, Stacy.

🏵 *Dive*. **Dutton, 1994.** [J] [S]

Fifteen-year-old Virginia's life seems to be unraveling one person at a time. Her father is dying of a blood disease, leaving her alcoholic mother distressed and distant. Her best friend Eileen is acting strangely, and she's not close to her older siblings. The one shining spot in Virginia's life is Jane, who is popular, passionate, and sure of herself. Virginia and Jane's friendship turns to romance, and from there things in Virginia's life start to look up a little: She begins to repair her relationship with her older sister, and her mother's behavior starts to make a little sense. (L)

Awards/honors: BBYA; Lambda Literary Award winner

Friend, Natasha.

Lush. **Scholastic, 2006.** [M] [J]

Thirteen-year-old Samantha struggles to hold her life together while keeping the destructive secret of her father's alcoholism. She turns to an anonymous friend to help, and she and her friend correspond by leaving each other notes in dusty library books. Although she is convinced that her friend is the cool girl studying at a far table, the friend turns out to be a boy named Jesse, who is hiding his own secret. He's gay, and now Samantha is the only one who knows. They give each other the strength to confront the fears behind their secrets. (G)

Lynch, Chris.

Blue-Eyed Son Trilogy. [S]

Dog Eat Dog. HarperCollins, 1996.

Mick runs away from his Boston home to escape his parents and his delinquent, drunk older brother Terry. The fifteen-year-old ends up in bed with his friend Toy's mother. Toy's father throws him out, and

Mick moves in temporarily with his friend Sully. To finally triumph over Terry, Mick trains a dog to fight. Of course the dog fight ends tragically, and Mick runs away with his gay friend Toy in search of a better life. (G)

Mick. HarperCollins, 1996.

Blood Relations. HarperCollins, 1996.

McMahon, Jennifer.

My Tiki Girl. **Dutton, 2008.** **J** **S**

Since breaking her leg in a car crash two years before the book opens, tenth-grader Maggie, formerly popular, feels like she has no identity. To remedy this, she ingratiates herself into the life of her new poetry-reading classmate, Dahlia, aka Tiki. Maggie finds herself developing sexual feelings for Tiki. The two create their own fantasy world, complete with nicknames, and form a band with two classmates. If she wants to return to her "normal" life pre-accident, though, Maggie will have to draw herself away from her relationship with Tiki.

Keywords: historical setting

Nolan, Han.

A Face in Every Window. **Harcourt Brace, 1999.** **J** **S**

Upon his grandmother's death, James Patrick (JP) is thrust into the role of parenting his developmentally disabled father and his unstable mother. His mother enters a contest and wins ownership of a decrepit farmhouse in New Hope, Pennsylvania. The family moves to the farmhouse, which becomes a sort of commune, a haven for free spirits and those who wander but are not necessarily lost. One of the farmhouse's residents is Larry, whose father has kicked him out of the house for being gay. Amid the chaos of people coming and going and his mother dating, JP is a pillar of stability. (G)

Ryan, P. E.

Saints of Augustine. **HarperTeen, 2007.** **J** **S**

One year after former best friends Sam and Charlie, both sixteen, stop speaking to each other, they reunite at a neighborhood park. Their lives resemble two halves of a whole. Charlie's mom is dead, and Sam's father has moved away, supposedly to research his book. During the year they spent apart, Sam found himself attracted to his gay friend but was unable to admit his feelings to himself or anyone else. He also had the added stress of dealing with his mother's homophobic boyfriend. Charlie cared for his alcoholic father and turned to pot as an escape. (G)

Trujillo, Carla.

What Night Brings. **Curbstone Press, 2003.** **S** **A/YA**

In the 1960s, eleven-year-old Marci is both a keeper of and surrounded by secrets. Her father, an alcoholic who cheats on her mother, is physically abusive, but her mother is unwilling to see his faults. Her uncle is gay, and Marci herself is starting to realize that she may be a lesbian, praying that she might become a boy so she can pursue the girl she has a crush on. Marci tells her coming-of-age story in a strong, spirited voice. (G, L)

Keywords: 1960s

Vande Velde, Vivian.

Alison, Who Went Away. **Houghton Mifflin, 2001.** **M** **J**

Fourteen-year-old Susan, who prefers to be called Sibyl, wants everyone to think that her biggest problem is getting a date for the upcoming dance, a problem she and her best friend plan to remedy by getting roles in a play at the local all-boys high school. As the book progresses, however, readers learn that Susan's family is harboring many dark secrets. Her father, who is gay, left when she was five. Her mother is overprotective and high strung. Her sister Alison disappeared from home three years ago and hasn't communicated with the family since then. (G)

Chapter 4

Genre Fiction

This chapter covers genre fiction, with the exception of romance, which is covered in chapter 2. The sections on genre fiction are shorter than the sections covering realistic fiction because not as many YA-specific books with GLBTQ characters are available. The appearance of GLBTQ genre titles is becoming more common, but in the meantime many of these books are adult titles with YA appeal. Science fiction and fantasy have one major advantage over realistic fiction: They can build their own worlds with their own rules, worlds in which homosexuality can be anything from verboten to mainstream.

Most of the YA books in this section feature secondary rather than main characters that are GLBTQ. Thanks to the success of J. K. Rowling's <u>Harry Potter</u> series, publishers know that more teens are happy to read long, involved fantasy novels. Urban fantasy has also grown in popularity, with faeries, vampires, and other supernatural creatures living among humans in cities and suburbs. Due to the growing presence and acceptance of GLBTQ characters in YA literature, plus the popularity of fantasy as a genre with teens, this subgenre should grow in the years to come.

Note: More genre fiction can be found in chapter 6. Keywords identifying the genre are listed at the ends of the entries. For other titles in specific genres, check the subject index.

Historical Fiction

"A long time ago in a far, far away land . . ." might be one of the best ways to define historical fiction. For the purposes of this guide, historical fiction includes any book that is set in a time period before the book was written. In some cases, the historical setting provides a backdrop for a character's attitude toward his or her own sexuality or that of other people. Authors may also choose a historical setting to show what coming-of-age was like in a different decade. These are not the only books with historical settings that appear in this guide; others are noted with the keywords "historical setting." In these books, however, the historical setting and narration of historical events takes narrative priority over other themes, such as the characters' sexuality.

Chambers, Aidan.

🎗 *Postcards from No Man's Land.* **Dutton, 2002.** **S**

Two stories—one set in the 1990s, and the other in the 1940s—weave together in this richly textured novel. Seventeen-year-old Jacob Todd travels from London to Amsterdam to attend a memorial service for his grandfather, also named Jacob Todd, who died fighting in World War II, and meet the family who sheltered him from the Nazis. Telling Jacob about his family history in the 1990s is his terminally ill grandmother, Geertrui, who relates how she and the first Jacob fell in love in Amsterdam despite Jacob's having a family back home in England. Through the course of the book, love and sexuality are important themes, as Jacob is interested in both a boy and a girl. (B)

Awards/honors: BBYA; Printz Award winner

Keywords: 1940s; Nazis; World War II

Jinks, Catherine.

Pagan Chronicles series. **S**

Pagan's Crusade: Book One of the Pagan Chronicles. Candlewick, 2003.

Pagan in Exile: Book Two of the Pagan Chronicles. Candlewick, 2004.

In the second book in this four-part series, Pagan is serving as squire to Lord Roland de Bram, whom he joined to escape a checkered past. The year is 1188, the setting is Jerusalem, and religious wars abound. Jerusalem has been overtaken by infidels, and Lord Roland returns to France to ask his family for their support in fighting for the city. Pagan expects that Lord Roland's family will be refined and well-mannered, but they are boorish and have no interest in the wars of other countries. One of Roland's brothers, Pagan learns, is gay, or "ganymede." (G)

Keywords: Middle Ages; Jerusalem

Pagan's Vows: Book Three of the Pagan Chronicles. Candlewick, 2005.

Pagan's Scribe: Book Four of the Pagan Chronicles. Candlewick, 2006.

Newbery, Linda.

The Shell House. **David Fickling Books, 2002.** **S**

The ruins of Graveney Hall, a home destroyed by fire in 1917, bring together two stories, one past and one present. In the present, Greg takes the opportunity to explore and photograph the grounds as he mulls over his romantic feelings for Jordan, a quiet but intelligent member of the school swim team. While exploring, Greg meets Faith, who is devoutly Christian. In the past, Edmund Pearson, who stands to inherit Graveney Hall, falls in love with Alex, a soldier, as World War I rages. Unfortunately, Edward is engaged, and his family wants him to produce an heir to the estate. (G)

Keywords: World War I

O'Neill, Jamie.

At Swim, Two Boys. **Scribner, 2003.** [A/YA]

Sixteen-year-old Jim, a privileged shopkeeper's son, and Doyler, poor but intelligent, make a pact to swim to an island in Dublin Bay in the summer of 1915. As they work toward their goal, they become romantically involved, and both cross paths with McMurrough, back in Ireland after serving prison time in England. By the next Easter, the day they were supposed to make their swim, Dublin is in the middle of a political uprising. Doyler is jailed for "sedition" and then becomes a volunteer soldier as war overtakes the city. (G)

Keywords: Ireland

Taylor, Kim.

Cissy Funk. **HarperCollins, 2001.** [M] [J]

During the Great Depression, thirteen-year-old Cissy lives with her abusive, moody mother and mostly absent older brother. Her aunt Vera, who is loving and compassionate, takes Cissy to live with her father in Denver after she sees the bruises on Cissy's body. Unfortunately, Cissy's father does not want any part of raising her, and she must return to her mother's home. Cissy learns that Vera, who is in a lesbian relationship, is really her mother and was forced to give Cissy up to be raised by her brother (the man Cissy thought was her father) and his wife. (L)

Keywords: Great Depression

Paranormal

When ghosts, spirits, werewolves, vampires, and other supernatural creatures show up in our normal world, the story can be defined as "paranormal." Paranormal romance is a popular genre for both adults and young adults, often featuring a human female who falls in love with an otherworldly creature. Though paranormal books for young adults fly off the shelves, not too many of them focus on, or even involve, gay and lesbian relationships, but here are a few.

Berman, Steve.

Vintage: A Ghost Story. **Haworth Press, 2007.** [S]

The ghost story is familiar to many: A hitchhiking figure dressed in clothing from decades past walks the highway, usually in the rainy autumn, looking for a ride. But this ghost, Josh, leaves the highway to follow the Goth narrator, who attends funerals and uses his Ouija board in the hope that he'll find something to live for. Josh's attraction to the living boy takes the reader to cemeteries and through the Goth culture. After his suicide attempt, the narrator starts to rebuild a support network, including his best friend Trace, her little brother Second Mike, and his Aunt Jan, who gives him shelter. (G)

Golden, Christopher.

Poison Ink. **Bantam Dell, 2008.** **S**

High school junior Sammi and her four closest friends are social floaters at school. Katsuko is the athlete; Simone, aka TQ, is the intellectual beauty; Letty is the out lesbian who flouts the social lines; and Caryn is the fashionista. The five of them agree to get matching tattoos as a symbol of their friendship. Sammi backs out at the last minute, and a day later all her friends shun her. They also exhibit strange, violent behavior, which Sammi learns is due to the tattoos magically expanding and taking over her friends' bodies. (L)

McLaughlin, Lauren.

Cycler. **Random House, 2008.** **S**

It's PMS at its worst. Everyone at school is convinced that seventeen-year-old Jill is completely average, a girl whose biggest concern is getting the guy she likes to take her to the prom. Four days before Jill gets her period, however, she turns into Jack, a typical teenage boy with all the typical teenage boy parts. Jack even has his own developed sexuality. Once Jack turns back into Jill, it's back to school for Jill as if nothing has happened. To further complicate matters, both Jack and Jill have romantic interests of their own. (B, Q)

Pearce, Jackson.

As You Wish. **HarperCollins, 2009.** **J**

Viola has just received the worst news ever: Her boyfriend, Lawrence, who is also her longtime friend, is gay. Devastated by Lawrence's news, Viola wishes she could just disappear. Then Jinn, a genie, appears and offers to make Viola's wishes come true. It sounds simple enough, but Viola is terrified that she'll make the wrong wishes. To further complicate her situation, Viola and Jinn are falling in love, and Jinn isn't so sure that he wants to go back to his homeland of Caliban. (G)

Fantasy

Though fantasy works often involve creatures that could just as easily show up in the "paranormal" category, fantasy books are distinguished from the paranormal books by virtue of their otherworldly settings. Urban fantasy generally takes place in cities that may be familiar to readers, but it also involves an unfamiliar place such as underground faerie courts. In fantasy, as opposed to science fiction, wondrous events occur because of magic, not because of science. Fantasy remains a popular genre with teens.

Black, Holly.

🌳 *Tithe*. **Simon & Schuster, 2002.** **J** **S**

This retelling of *Tam Lin* centers on sixteen-year-old Kaye, whose mother narrowly escapes being murdered in Philadelphia. Back at her grandmother's house in coastal New Jersey, Kaye reunites with her best friend Janet and Janet's brother Corny, who is gay. Kaye has known all her life that faeries are real, and now she is faced with two problems. First, she is a changeling, slowly turning into a faery, complete with use of magic. Second, the faeries of the evil Unseelie court plan to sacrifice her as their tithe to Hell, which they must pay in order to remain free. (G)

Awards/honors: BBYA; Teens Top Ten selection

Keywords: faery

Ironside: A Modern Faery's Tale. **(Sequel). Simon & Schuster, 2007.** **S**

Kaye's love Roiben now rules the Unseelie court. To prove her devotion to Roiben, Kaye pledges herself as his consort and must complete a near-impossible task. Corny continues to suffer from a faery curse. Kaye also confesses to her mother that she is a faery, which horrifies her mother. After the fight with her mother, Kaye returns to the faery courts. She, Corny, and two brothers they meet (who appear in Black's novel *Valiant,* Simon & Schuster, 2005) become pawns in a war between the faeries. (G)

Keywords: faery

Brennan, Herbie.

Faerie Wars series.

Faerie Wars. Bloomsbury USA, 2003. **M** **J**

After his mother admits to having an affair with his father's secretary, fourteen-year-old Henry Atherton's family life is a mess. To escape the tension leading to his parents' imminent breakup, Henry performs chores for his neighbor, Mr. Fogarty. Meanwhile, Prince Pyrgus Malvae is running for his life from the Faerie world, where the Faeries of the Night are trying to kill him. Their paths cross when Pyrgus Malvae arrives through a portal into Henry's world and ends up under the lawn mower at Mr. Fogarty's house. Together with Pyrgus's sister, Henry and Pyrgus work together to return Pyrgus to the Faerie realm. (L)

Awards/honors: BBYA

The Purple Emperor. Bloomsbury, 2006. **M** **J**

Henry has left his family problems behind in the human world, but a new set of problems awaits. The reluctant royal Pyrgus is set to become emperor, but villains are hunting him. Pyrgus's rival, Hairstreak, would rather see Pyrgus's weaker brother, Comma, on the throne. Henry helps Pyrgus and his sister, Holly Blue, defeat Hairstreak. Love also abounds: Henry and Holly share a kiss, and Pyrgus finds a romance of his own.

Ruler of the Realm. Bloomsbury, 2007. **M** **J**

Holly Blue now rules the Faerie realm. She receives an offer of a truce from Hairstreak, but she's suspicious about whether the offer is real. To find out, she travels to a local soothsayer to see if she can learn the future of her realm. Prince Pyrgus discovers crystal flowers that may prove to be a powerful weapon for his people. Once Henry returns to the Faerie realm, the spark of love between him and Holly magnifies.

The Faerie Lord. Bloomsbury, 2008. **M** **J**

Henry spends two years trying to forget the Faerie realm, but finds doing so impossible. While he is taking care of Mr. Fogarty's home, Pyrgus returns. Pyrgus is suffering from a plague that is causing many residents of Faerie to age at an accelerated rate. To help save Faerie, Henry returns to the realm, where he embarks on a lonely journey that takes him far away from the palace he knows.

Clare, Cassandra.

Mortal Instruments trilogy.

The Mortal Instruments: City of Bones. Simon & Schuster, 2007. **J** **S**

On the night her mother Jocelyn disappears, fifteen-year-old Clary finds out that she has a legacy with a group of otherworldly beings who call themselves Shadowhunters. Her guide in the Shadowhunters is Jace Wayland, who lives with fellow Shadowhunters Alec and Isabel. The Shadowhunters' search for Jocelyn and the truth of Clary's identity takes them to underground parties and abandoned hotels in New York. As Clary, through Jace, discovers more about her Shadowhunter legacy, Alec's attraction to Jace and his jealousy of Clary and her friend Simon threatens their operation. (G)

City of Ashes. Simon & Schuster, 2008. **J** **S**

Clary is now fully entrenched in the world of the Shadowhunters. She still hasn't found her mother, and her father, the evil and seemingly omnipotent Valentine, might hold the clues to her mother's disappearance. Though she'd like to return to the real world to spend more time with her friend Simon, who is well on his way to becoming more than a friend, Jace and the Shadowhunter world keep a strong hold on her.

City of Glass. Simon & Schuster, 2009. **J** **S**

To find a potion that will save her mother, Clary must use her unrefined powers to summon an angel, who one way or another will end the battle among the opposing sides of the Moon, the Night, and Faerie. In fact, saving much of the world rests on Clary's shoulders, because she must enter the ancient City of Glass without permission, an act that could cost her her life.

Donoghue, Emma.

Kissing the Witch: Old Tales in New Skins. **HarperCollins, 1997.** **S**

Moving forward with the ideas of violence and darkness behind many traditional fairy tales, Donoghue retells the stories everyone knows but with a feminist twist. The language is much more lyrical and literary than most fairy tale retellings, and each story is linked by the last line of the one before it: "Who were you before . . . ." The familiar characters, like Snow White and Gretel, retell their stories of shallow, worthless princes and find their worth and identity in the things that make outsiders identify them as witches. (L)

Keywords: fairy tales; retellings; short stories

Lackey, Mercedes.

Magic's Pawn : Last Herald Mage Trilogy Book 1. DAW Books, 1989. **A/YA**
The last herald mage of the title is Vanyel, who travels to the Royal Court of Valdemar to receive instruction from his aunt Savil on the ways of royalty and fighting evil. His father hopes that Vanyel will become more masculine under Savil's tutelage. While coming of age in the royal court, Vanyel begins a romance with another boy, Tylendal. Along with this romance, Vanyel also learns what it means to be strong, and about the not-always-obvious divide between good and evil. (G)

Lo, Malinda.

Ash. Little, Brown, 2009. **S**
This retelling of "Cinderella" centers around Ash, who takes comfort in reading her favorite fairy tales by the fire. Her father and mother are dead, and she is living at the mercy of her cruel stepmother. Ash wishes that the fairies in her stories would steal her, the way they do in changeling lore. She meets a fairy and believes that her wish will be granted. Then Ash meets Kaisa, a hunter for the king. Learning to hunt with Kaisa gives Ash's life new meaning, but soon she must decide between her love for Kaisa and her longtime dreams of a fairy-tale life. (L)

Keywords: fairy tales; retellings

Pierce, Tamora.

Will of the Empress. Scholastic, 2005. **J**
Mages Sandry, Tris, Daja, and Briar from Pierce's <u>The Circle Opens</u> and <u>The Circle of Magic</u> series reunite in this follow-up book. Now sixteen, they have grown apart over the two years before the opening of the book. Sandry holds some lands in trust for the Empress, and she learns that these lands will be given to someone else unless she returns home. She asks her three friends to accompany her, and as they travel and fight enemies, their bond grows stronger. One story line deals with Daja's sexuality; she describes herself as a "woman who loves women." (L)

Science Fiction

Ordinary teens who obtain superpowers from radioactive spider bites become superheroes. A man figures out how to travel at light speed and changes the fate of the world. A disease wipes out everyone on the planet save for the population of a small town. These scenarios and more are science fiction, in which writers create worlds that stem from ideas about the scientific world we already know. In science fiction, the characters, both good and bad, remain solidly human even if genetically modified.

Moore, Perry.

🏅 *Hero*. **Hyperion, 2007.** 🟦 🟦

High schooler Thom Creed's father, Hal, was once a member of The League, revered for his strength and superpowers, until an accident damages his hand and makes him an outcast. Thom has his own problems to deal with, too. His own superpowers are emerging, and he has to work hard at keeping his sexual orientation under wraps. His ability to heal earns him an invitation to audition for the position of hero's apprentice. This job, however, is taken from him when he must reveal that he's gay. (G)

Awards/honors: Lambda Literary Award winner

Gerrold, David.

Starsider Trilogy.

Jumping off the Planet. Tor, 2000. **A/YA**

Thirteen-year-old Charles, aka Chigger, a middle child, never gets the attention he wants from his parents. In the twenty-first century, Earth is overcrowded, and its residents have to travel to the moon and planets beyond just to have a place to live. Even off the planet, disease and crime still plague Earth's residents. Chigger and his brothers (one of whom is gay) are kidnapped by their white-collar criminal father and chased by their lesbian mother across the interplanetary travel systems and social networks. (G, L)

Bouncing off the Moon. Tor, 2002. **A/YA**

Chigger and his brothers have resolved to stay together through their parents' divorce. They leave Earth, but even with the assistance of a known money launderer, the trip off Earth to the moon is perilous. Chigger's younger brother holds onto a robot monkey, a toy that is much more advanced than it seems. Are their travels really that dangerous, or is someone trying to murder them?

Leaping to the Stars. Tor, 2003. **A/YA**

Aided by an artificial intelligence called HARLIE, which is built into his younger brother's toy monkey, Chigger and his family seek a new home. To escape a predatory government, they sign on to colonize an outlying planet, where the only thing they can be sure of is hard labor day in and day out. Though the family is on their way to potential freedom, they have to protect themselves from a group who believe that HARLIE is an object of evil.

Griffith, Nicola.

Slow River. **Del Rey, 1995.** **A/YA**

This follow-up to Griffith's *Ammonite* (Del Rey, 1992; Lambda Literary Award winner) follows Lore van Osterling, an heiress who escapes kidnappers, as she is taken in by a woman named Spanner. Together, Lore and Spanner scam rich people in futuristic, slightly dystopian Europe. Lore falls for Spanner, but ultimately their relationship does not last. Lore leaves her heiress life permanently to work in a water-treatment plant, establishing her own identity outside of her family as well as Spanner. The author uses first- and third-person narration to convey the passage of time and reflection on the part of the narrator. (L)

Mystery

At its most basic, a mystery sets up a crime, and the protagonist solves it. Not every mystery has to involve a serious crime like murder or kidnapping, though the ones highlighted in this section do just that.

Hamilton, R. J.

Who Framed Lorenzo Garcia? **Pride Pack, No. 1. Alyson Publications, 1995.** **S**

Kicked out of his home after coming out to his father, Ramon Torres lives in foster homes and on the streets. He is taken in by a gay cop, Officer Garcia, who wants to adopt him. Before that can happen, unscrupulous police officers, whom Garcia was going to report for drug use, frame Garcia as a drug dealer. While living in his newest home, Ramon musters the Pride Pack, his friends from the local Gay & Lesbian Center, to help clear Garcia's name. (G)

Rice, Christopher.

Light Before Day. **Miramax, 2005.** **A/YA**

Twenty-six-year-old Adam is a journalist looking for his big break. While working for a gay men's magazine and living in West Hollywood, Adam discovers what he thinks might be a murder mystery involving a closeted Marine and a pedophilic pimp. With the help of a mystery novelist, Adam uncovers three other unsolved murders of gay men thought to be the victims of a serial killer. The investigation costs Adam his magazine job, but he has more important things to worry about when his ex-boyfriend goes missing. (G)

Chapter 5

Alternative Formats

Visually appealing and often easier to read, formats other than the standard novel have become wildly popular with teens. Generation Y and the generations after it grew up in a visual world, often using multimedia teaching tools and learning via television and the Internet. They are accustomed to multitasking when they read, using words and pictures together to form an entire idea. Comics and graphic novels, books told in comic format, no longer carry the stigma of being "just for kids" or "just for geeks." This visual way of reading is enjoyed by everyone. As author Neil Gaiman famously said, *Graphic novels are a format, not a genre*. Graphic novels can tell any story for any audience. One popular publishing trend is graphic novelizations of best sellers.

Poetry and verse are also perpetually popular formats with teens. Many teens write poetry of their own, and YALSA encourages young adult librarians to hold poetry workshops and readings for young writers. One of the best-selling poets in America in 2008 was Ellen Hopkins, who writes novels in verse that chronicle the lives of troubled teens. Writing poetry allows teen writers to express themselves in ways other than essays, which are often assigned for homework. Novels in verse always have lots of white space on the page, which appeals to reluctant readers. Poetry can form around the shapes of words, too, which gives the words and poems extra meaning to visual learners.

This chapter highlights books in formats other than the standard novel. First, poetry and novels in verse are covered. The next section includes graphic novels, and the last section is on manga (Japanese comics). (Poetry collections are covered in chapter 6.)

Poetry

Poetry delivers passion, intimacy, and brevity to teens, who often greatly enjoy reading (and writing in) this format. One important decision teen librarians must make when buying poetry is where to shelve it. Collected volumes of poetry are considered nonfiction and are usually shelved under Dewey Decimal Classification numbers 808 or 811. Novels in verse, however, should be shelved in fiction under the author's last name. The poetry listed here is separated from nonfiction books because of its format.

Cole, Rachel T., and Rita D. Costello, eds.

🌳 *Bend Don't Shatter: Poets on the Beginning of Desire.* **Soft Skull Press, 2004.** S A/YA

Fifty-nine poems cover many aspects of teen GLBTQ sexuality, from confusion to lust to being "totally freaked out." None of the poets is known for writing works for young adults, but the writing is of high quality, and teens will appreciate the honesty of their words and the wisdom the adult authors have gained in their lives. Many different styles of poetry are represented, as are many different viewpoints and stories of discovering and accepting sexuality. (GLBTQ)

Awards/honors: PPYA

Merrell, Billy.

Talking in the Dark. **Push, 2003.** S

In free verse poetry, Merrell, age twenty-five, writes a memoir about his parents' divorce when he was seven and his realization of his homosexuality. He writes with wisdom about his relationships with his parents, especially the aspect of those relationships that revolved around his sexuality. His comfort in his sexuality may offer solace to some readers; he writes that it is a part of him that he has always known. Other topics he covers, all discussed with sophistication, include death, friendships, and family relations. (G)

Novels in Verse

Poetry refers to collections of poems that can stand alone, even if they have an overarching theme. In verse novels, poems come together to make up a single complete story.

Frost, Helen.

🌳 *Keesha's House.* **Farrar, Straus & Giroux, 2003.** J S

Told in sestinas and sonnets, this book follows the lives of residents of a house for runaways and homeless teens. The owner of the house is not Keesha, but Joe, whose aunt took him in when he was a teen. Residents of the house include pregnant, frightened Stephie; sexual abuse survivor Keesha; and Harris, whose father threw him out when he came out as gay. Joe gives hope and stability to teens who have no place to go. Each character is distinct and well crafted, and the verse form of this book makes it especially appealing to budding poets. (G)

Awards/honors: BBYA; Printz Honor

Hopkins, Ellen.

Impulse. **Simon & Schuster, 2007.** J S

Tony, one of three narrators, tells his story of abandonment, abuse, and finding love when he's out on the streets. The book, told in verse, chronicles the lives of three teens in Aspen Springs, a mental health facility where they will learn to cope with their demons, including cutting, drug abuse, and bipolar disorder. Although Tony has a juvenile record, he is also shown to be a good listener and a loyal friend and is dedicated to succeeding in the recovery program. During his time in Aspen

Springs the reader learns of his dysfunctional relationship with his father and the one time in his life when he truly knew love. (G)

Koertge, Ron.

🏵 *The Brimstone Journals*. **Candlewick, 2001.** [S]

Fifteen students at Branston, aka Brimstone, High tell their personal stories of struggles with family, sexuality, anger, and racial identity in a collection of sparse, free verse poems. Kitty is anorexic, Tran feels he can never live up to his immigrant father's vision of success. Sheila has a crush on her best friend Monica, who doesn't reciprocate her feelings. Boyd is a white supremacist with an alcoholic father who acts, for the most part, as if Boyd doesn't exist. Boyd's anger and hatred build as he plans a school shooting, which is stopped at the last minute by some of his classmates. (L)

Awards/honors: BBYA; QP

Levithan, David.

🏵 *The Realm of Possibility*. **Knopf, 2004.** [S]

Twenty characters who all attend the same school tell stories of love, sex, friendship, and families in the form of verse and essays. Varying poetry and storytelling forms show each character's personality, and the book opens with Daniel's voice, which says, "My parents are okay with me being gay but they would kill me if they saw me with a cigarette." Diana writes love songs to Elizabeth, who doesn't know Diana likes her. This book also fits in well with books in the "Friends" and "Family" sections of chapter 2, as multiple perspectives are used. The mixed cast and alternate format will diversify any YA collection. (G, L)

Awards/honors: BBYA

Wolff, Virginia Euwer.

🏵 *True Believer*. **Atheneum, 2001.** [M] [J]

When LaVaughn's childhood friend Jody moves back to her neighborhood, she's glad to have Jody back. She's been drifting apart from her closest friends Myrtle and Annie, who decide to join "Cross Your Legs for Jesus," a club that LaVaughn finds too strict for her personal beliefs. Jody and LaVaughn attend a dance together, but she realizes their relationship can't be much more than platonic when she catches him kissing another boy. The story takes place against a backdrop of school problems in this is follow-up to Wolff's *Make Lemonade* (Holt, 1993). (G)

Awards/honors: BBYA; Printz Honor winner

Wyeth, Sharon Dennis.

Orphea Proud. **Delacorte, 2005.** [S]

Using poetry and an open mike to share the story of her life, seventeen-year-old Orphea Proud tells her story at Club Nirvana, a New York City café. Orphea is an orphan who fell in love with her best friend, who died the day after their first kiss. As well as her sexuality, Orphea talks about her relationship with her dead mother's family and her homophobic brother. The alternate format (in this case, poetry), may appeal to some more reluctant readers, and the African American characters add diversity. (L)

Graphic Novels

Bechdel, Alison.

Fun Home: A Family Tragicomic. **Houghton Mifflin, 2006.** **S** **A/YA**
Annotated in chapter 6.

Castellucci, Cecil, and Jim Rugg.

The Plain Janes. **DC Minx, 2007.** **M** **J** **S**
After Jane survives a sidewalk bombing in Metro City, her fearful mother and father move her to suburbia. The popular crowd wants Jane to join them, but she wants to be part of a less popular group of girls all named Jane (or Jayne, or Polly Jane), who bring a variety of interests and skills to their friendship. The Janes, who are accepting of the one openly gay kid in school, come up with the idea of creating a movement called People Loving Art In Neighborhoods, or PLAIN. Not everyone in town appreciates PLAIN's efforts to create art, however, and the group is labeled as dangerous. (G)

Janes in Love. **(Sequel). Minx, 2008.** **M** **J** **S**
The Janes aren't ready to give up their art, which thrills their high school classmates and enrages the more uptight residents of their town. It's February now, and everyone is looking for someone to love. Jane, however, keeps a clear head. She continues to correspond with Miroslaw, whose life she saved at the beginning of *The Plain Janes*. Wanting to reach others with her art in a way that might not have the police constantly hunting for her, Jane applies for a grant to build a corner garden that everyone in the town can enjoy.

Denson, Abby.

Tough Love: High School Confidential. **Manic D Press, 2006.** **S**
In this soap opera, roller-coaster high school romance, Brian is the new kid in town, Chris is the boy he likes, and Julie is their supportive friend. As Brian and Chris fall in love, they face the issues of Brian being assaulted by homophobic jocks, Brian's coming out to his mother (who is a little surprised, but ultimately supportive), suicide, and establishing sexuality. There are also happy moments when Brian and Chris can be alone as a couple. The art is similar to many manga titles and may appeal to fans of that genre. (G)

Gaiman, Neil.

Sandman Series.

Preludes and Nocturnes. DC Vertigo, 1989. **A/YA**

The Doll's House. DC Vertigo, 1991 **A/YA**

Dream Country. DC Vertigo, 1992. **A/YA**

A Season of Mists. DC Vertigo, 1992. **A/YA**

The Sandman: A Game of You. DC Vertigo, 1993. **A/YA**

This is the fifth volume in the eleven-volume <u>Sandman</u> collection. Barbie, a minor character in *The Doll's House,* gets her own story. She has broken up with her boyfriend Ken and moved into the city, where her neighbors in the tenement building include "Auntie" Wanda, a male-to-female transgender, and Hazel and Foxglove, a lesbian couple. When Barbie's life is threatened by a force from The Dreaming, her neighbors, helped by a centuries-old witch named Thessaly who is disguised as a college student, travel through her dreams to save her. (L, T)

Keywords: fantasy; short stories

Fables and Reflections. DC Vertigo, 1994. **A/YA**

Brief Lives. DC Vertigo, 1994. **A/YA**

World's End. DC Vertigo, 1999. **A/YA**

The Kindly Ones. DC Vertigo, 1999. **A/YA**

The Wake. DC Vertigo, 1999. **A/YA**

Endless Nights. DC Vertigo, 2003. **A/YA**

Moore, Alan, and José Villarrubia.

The Mirror of Love. **Top Shelf Productions, 2004.** **A/YA**

Graphic novel enthusiasts will recognize Moore's work (*The Watchmen, The League of Extraordinary Gentlemen*), but this is no superhero comic. This is a literary, thought-provoking look at the history of homosexuality, told as a poem between an anonymous writer and his or her amour. The prose and the pictures are meant to work together, like a picture book, and the pictures often respond to questions asked by the text. Many references to great writers and artists infuse the text, including Sappho, Emily Dickinson, and Oscar Wilde. (G, L)

Keywords: nonfiction

Moore, Terry.

🎗 *Strangers in Paradise Pocket Book 1.* **Abstract Studios, 2004.** **A/YA**

Katchoo is living a pretty good life. She's a talented artist and very much in love with her best friend, Francine. At an art museum, Katchoo meets David and the two begin a friendship. Despite Katchoo's protestations, David is interested in a relationship beyond friendship. The Katchoo-Francine-David love triangle, however, becomes a very minor worry for Katchoo compared to the Mafia catching up with her. The mob is missing $850,000, and Katchoo's former employer believes she's responsible for its disappearance. The strength of this book lies in its characterizations. (L)

Awards/honors: PPYA

Paluzzi, Mia.

Paintings of You. Iris Print, 2007. **S**

Claude is a well-known, talented painter, but photographer Benedict Connor knows the truth about Claude's work: It's technically beautiful but has no passion. Ben is determined to help Claude find emotion in his work. At art college, Claude falls for Ben, but Claude's roommate Hero and Hero's boyfriend are convinced that Claude is interested in Ben's best friend Beatrice. A Shakespearean-style comedy of errors ensues as everyone tries to help Claude win Beatrice's heart . . . except Claude himself. In the end, Claude and Ben do get together and kiss. (G)

Tamaki, Mariko, and Jilliam Tamaki.

🏆 *Skim.* Groundwood, 2008. **S**

Kim, nicknamed Skim "because I'm not," chronicles a season in her life in her diary. Her best friend Lisa is invited to become a part of the popular clique, which only complicates goth Wiccan Kim's quest for self. She develops a crush on a female teacher, which leads her to question her sexuality. At the same time, she grows closer to a classmate whose ex-boyfriend commits suicide. (L)

Awards/honors: BBYA; GGNT

Van Meter, Jen, Christine Norrie, and Chynna Clugston.

Hopeless Savages series.

Hopeless Savages. Oni Press, 2002. **S**

Despite the title, the main characters in this book are not criminals. Dirk Hopeless and Nikki Savage are suburban relics from the 1970s punk scene who are raising their four children: corporate, Gap-wearing Rat Bastard; goth Arsenal Fierce; mod Twitch Strummer; and the series protagonist, Skank Zero. Twitch is gay and dating Arsenal's boyfriend's younger brother, and their relationship and trip to Hong Kong are a focus of the third volume in the series. (G)

Ground Zero. Oni Press, 2004. **S**

Too Much Hopeless. Oni Press, 2004. **S**

Vaughan, Brian K.

Ex Machina series.

The First Hundred Days. DC Wildstorm, 2005. **S**

🏆 *Tag.* DC Wildstorm, 2005. **S** **A/YA**

Mitchell Hundred survived an explosion only to find that he has acquired the ability to communicate with and control machines. He's now mayor of New York, and in the aftermath of September 11 he's been forced to reveal his identity. At the same time that he's dealing with a serial killer in the subways who is leaving clues to the explosion that gave him his powers, he's taking heat from the press and his constituents because he's openly in favor of same-sex marriage, even officiating at the wedding ceremony of two men. (G)

Awards/honors: GGNT

Keywords: science fiction; superheroes

Fact v. Fiction. DC Wildstorm, 2006. **S**

March to War. DC Wildstorm, 2006. **S**

Smoke, Smoke. DC Wildstorm, 2007. **S**

Power Down. DC Wildstorm, 2007. **S**

Y: The Last Man series.

🎗 *Unmanned.* DC Vertigo, 2003. **A/YA**

The Y in the series name is Yorick Brown, an escape artist who has a terrific girlfriend and a loving if not perfect family. Then a plague wipes out every living male thing on Earth, from cows to humans, and the only Y chromosome carriers to survive are Yorick and his trained monkey, Ampersand. Yorick doesn't know why he survived, but he believes that now his job is to save humanity. (L)

Awards/honors: PPYA

Keywords: science fiction

Cycles. DC Vertigo, 2003. **A/YA**

One Small Step. DC Vertigo, 2003. **A/YA**

Safeword. DC Vertigo, 2004. **A/YA**

Ring of Truth. DC Vertigo, 2005. **A/YA**

Girl on Girl. DC Vertigo, 2005. **A/YA**

Paper Dolls. DC Vertigo, 2006. **A/YA**

Kimono Dragons. DC Vertigo, 2006. **A/YA**

Motherland. DC Vertigo, 2007. **A/YA**

Winick, Judd.

🎗 *Green Lantern: Brother's Keeper.* **DC Comics, 2003. S A/YA**

Winick tackles homophobia in this installment in the long-running superhero comic series. Green Lantern's enemy Brainwave returns in an opening action sequence, bringing chaos to the city via mind manipulation. Brainwave leaves but promises Green Lantern, aka Kyle, that he will return. Kyle, a graphic artist, and his girlfriend Jennifer head for his hometown, but when he arrives he learns that his assistant, Terry, is in a coma after being beaten by homophobes. Dismayed by the dark side of humanity, Green Lantern is able to track down and find all those responsible for Terry's beating. Includes an afterword. (G)

Awards/honors: PPYA

Keywords: science fiction; superheroes

Manga

Manga is a collective term for Japanese comics. Many of these comics are serialized and/or based on popular, animated Japanese television shows. Manga has a distinct style; it's usually printed in black-and-white and often appears to be bound backward. Because Japanese is written right to left, the opposite of English, American publishers who brought manga to the United States often had problems with the translation and placement of the text in relation to the pictures. To solve this problem, they started binding manga to read, even in English, from right to left. Manga is packaged in smaller trim sizes than novels and sells at a lower price point, averaging about $10 for a paperback volume.

Manga also has a very fast rate of production, with many new series coming out each year. Those annotated in this section are proven favorites of readers and librarians. Most are multivolume series; whether to buy an entire series or just a few volumes is up to individual collection developers.

Gotoh, Shinobu.

Time Lag. **Digital Manga Publishing, 2006.** **S** **A/YA**

Every year, feminine-looking Saturo tells his best friend Shioru that he has a crush on him, and every year he is rejected. Saturo's best guess as to why Shioru continually rejects his advances is that Shioru is in love with their (male) classmate Seiichi. What Saturo doesn't know is that Seiichi is in love with him. Confusion reigns over their almost-love triangle until a letter arrives at Saturo's house three years after it was mailed. This is a stand-alone volume, making it a good choice for libraries that want to buy books in the genre but don't have the money to invest in an ongoing series. (G)

Higuri, You.

Gorgeous Carat Galaxy. **Digital Manga Publishing, 2006.** **S**

This is a one-volume, less explicit continuation of the four-part Gorgeous Carat (Blu, 2006), a historical action and romance series set in early twentieth-century Paris. Noir is a jewel thief. Florian, who has amethyst eyes, is payment for a debt owed to Noir by his noble but poor family. Since then they have kept constant company. At a castle surrounded by "the forest of the sacred beast," they come upon a murder mystery. Florian is in danger, and it's up to Noir to protect him. (G)

Kannagi, Saturo.

Rin! **Digital Manga Publishing, 2006.** **J** **S**

Archery is the favorite activity of longtime friends Katsura and Sou (who is also Katsura's older brother's best friend). Katsura's greatest aspiration is to be as good at archery as his brother Yamato, who captains the school archery team. His nerves, however, are his downfall. The only person who can calm him down is Sou. As they've grown older, Sou has distanced himself from Katsura, citing discomfort. Without Sou's hugs, Katsura's archery skills suffer, and another classmate offers to be the hug-giver. It's not until this third party steps in that Katsura and Suo think about their true feelings for each other. (G)

Kannagi, Satoru, and Hotaru Odagiri.

Only the Ring Finger Knows series. **S**

🏆 *The Lonely Ring Finger.* Digital Manga Publishing, 2006.

The "it" fad at Wataru Fujii's high school is rings. Students wear rings that match the ones owned by their significant others. Following the fad, second-year student Wataru wears a ring even though he is single. He accidentally switches rings with popular, kind third-year student Yuichi Kazuki. Yuichi does not react to the switch with his usual kindness, starting a conflicted, complicated relationship revolving around the switched rings. All at once, Yuichi and Wataru are enemies, friends, and interested in one another, even potential soul mates. (G)

Awards/honors: PPYA

The Left Hand Dreams of Him. Digital Manga Publishing, 2006.

The Ring Finger Falls Silent. Digital Manga Publishing, 2006.

Kawai, Chigusa.

La Esperança. **Digital Manga Publishing, 2005. S**

Georges Saphir is a good student and popular among his classmates at his European school. His worry about becoming like his domineering father, however, ensures that he is not close to anyone. His protective shell begins to break when Robert Jade, the headmaster's insightful, felonious son, enters his life. Robert, both fascinated and repulsed by Georges, seems determined to make his life miserable. After a near-fatal incident in a cathedral, Georges learns Robert's secret from a classmate: Georges resembles a girl Robert once loved, whose death Robert feels responsible for. There are seven volumes in the series . (G)

Kouga, Yun.

Earthian, Vol. 1. **BLU, 2005. S A/YA**

For millennia angels have watched over and lived among humans, whom they call the "Earthians." Lately the Earthians have greatly displeased the Archangel Michael, who threatens to destroy humanity when he finds 10,000 "minuses" about it. Angels Chihaya and Kagetsuya have grudgingly been granted permission to count humanity's "pluses" to balance out the minuses, and they're dealing with their own sexual tension. Earthians, however, might be the least of the angels' worries: A disease is spreading among the legion of angels, and their hope for survival lies with a fallen angel, Lord Seraphim. There are five volumes in the Earthian series. (G)

Keywords: fantasy; graphic format

Matoh, Sanami.

🏆 *Fake, Vol. 1.* **Tokyopop, 2003. S**

This popular *shonen-ai* series in seven parts focuses on NYPD officers Ryo and Dee, who work together in the 27th Precinct. Dee is gay and has a crush on Ryo, but puts his feelings aside temporarily when the two of them are assigned to investigate the murder of a drug mule. Dee and the son of the mule, Bikky, are kidnapped, and it's up to Ryo to rescue them. Ryo and Dee fight and solve crimes, and their relationship is fraught with humor, sexual tension, and the meddling of secondary characters Bikky, Carol, and J.J. There are seven volumes in the Fake series. (G)

Awards/honors: PPYA

Keywords: mystery

Matushita, Yoko.

Descendants of Darkness. **VIZ, 2006.** S A/YA

Asato Tsuzuki is a *shinigami,* a god of death. At age thirteen, Hisoka Kurosaki was cursed with a death that took three years to complete. He is also a *shingami,* and Tsuzuki's partner in business, where his empathy and introversion serve as a foil to Tsuzuki's hot-headedness. The two begin a relationship. Together they fight a common enemy, the evil Kazutaka Muraki, who is obsessed with Tsuzuki and commits crimes against Kurosaki. There are eleven volumes in the Descendants of Darkness series. (G)

Keywords: paranormal

Mitzushiro, Setona.

After School Nightmare. **Go! Comic, 2005.** A/YA

Mashiro Ichijo, the hottest boy in school, is hiding an unusual secret: From the waist up he is male, but he is female from the waist down. When asked, he tells others that he is male, but lately he's begun to doubt himself. He's not sure whether he wants to live as a man or a woman. The "nightmare" is that he has to compete against his classmates in a world of dreams as part of a special class, and his classmates can alter their appearance and physical abilities. (Q)

Keywords: paranormal

Miyagi, Tooko.

Il Gatto Sul G. **Digital Manga Publishing, 2006.** S

Riyi Narukawa's talent for the violin brings him angst, not pleasure. He purposely injures his hand to avoid playing, and in his pain ends up collapsing on Atsushi Ikeda's front doorstep. Atsushi is a nice guy, maybe too nice, who takes Riyi in for the night and watches over him while his hand heals. Atsushi becomes a sort of refuge for Riyi, who in addition to his violin woes is being pursued by a senior at his school in whom he's not interested, and who has a personality disorder. There are three volumes in the Il Gatto Sul G series. (G)

Murakami, Maki.

Gravitation. **Tokyopop, 2003.** S

Wannabe rock star Shuichi Shindo doesn't let his lack of talent or music industry experience deter him from writing songs and practicing with his best friend. Eiri Yuki is a well-known romance novelist who also happens to have an ear for music.

Eiri, mysterious and beautiful, harshly criticizes Shuichi's work, but instead of being driven away, Shuichi wants to know more about Eiri. Shuichi ingrains himself in Eiri's life, determined to prove that he's not the amateur no-talent Eiri believes him to be. Fate would say that their futures are entwined, but Eiri doesn't believe in fate. Really. There are twelve volumes in the Gravitation series. (G)

Shiozu, Shuri.

Eerie Queerie, Vol. 1. **Tokyopop, 2004.** S

This four-part series centers on ghost-whispering high school student Mitsuo Shiozu. Spirits often take over Mitsuo's body to resolve unfinished problems from their lives on Earth. In volume one, he is possessed by a girl who had a crush on his classmate Hasunuma, and while possessed he professes his—meaning her—love for Hasunuma. This leads his classmates to believe he's gay, and although he doesn't think he is, he does develop feelings for Hasunama, whose knowledge of ghosts enables Mitsuo to take his body back from his possessor. Other possessions by female spirits lead to gender-bending high jinks. (G, Q)

Keywords: paranormal

Takaguchi, Satosumi.

Shout Out Loud! **BLU, 2006.** S

Shino works as a *seiyuu,* an anime voice actor. Seventeen years ago, he fell in love with a woman, but they broke up when she became pregnant with his child. After she dies, their son, Nakaya, whom Shino has never met, comes to live with him. Shino is desperate for work so he can care for Nakaya and takes a job voicing romantic scenes in boys love movies. Voicing the scenes is awkward for him at first, but he is helped by a colleague, Tenryu, who is interested in Shino as more than just a coworker. There are five volumes in the series. (G)

Yoshinaga, Fuji.

Antique Bakery. **Digital Manga Publishing, 2002.** J S

Yusuke Ono is a pastry chef with a curse: His "Demonically Gay Charm" keeps him from working any one job too long. Ono can make any man fall for him, regardless of the other man's sexuality. The one person immune to his charm, though, is Keisuke Tachibana, the owner of Antique Bakery and a former schoolmate who rejected Ono's advances. Other employees of the bakery include Eiji Kanda, Ono's apprentice, who used to be a boxer until detached retinas made him quit, and Chikage Kobayakawa, the son of Tachibana's housekeeper, who has what he believes is an unrequited crush on Ono. There are four volumes in the series. (G)

Awards/honors: GGNT

Yumeka, Sumomo.

Same Cell Organism. **Digital Manga Publishing, 2006.** **J** **S**

This is a collection of four stories in seven chapters. Each story, centered on first re-lationships and romances, is about a different set of characters and can stand alone. In one story, two classmates inspire each other to succeed and find that their close friendship has turned to love. Another tells the story of a boy who falls in love with an angel. The artwork is simple yet vivid, and due to the more inno-cent content (it doesn't go beyond kissing), it may be an appropriate choice for younger readers. (G)

Chapter 6

GLBTQ Nonfiction

Don't overlook the importance of providing quality, high-interest nonfiction to GLBTQ teens and those interested in reading about GLBTQ issues. First, keep in mind that nonfiction is popular among both avid and reluctant readers. Nonfiction often comes in unusual trim sizes and colors, sometimes with full-color photography, visual aspects that all readers can appreciate. Second, reading biographies and autobiographies and hearing stories by and from those who've "been there" may reassure some readers who are questioning their sexuality or contemplating coming out to their friends and family.

GLBTQ Voices and Life Stories

The focus in this section is on real GLBTQ characters, how they live and feel (or lived and felt), and what they have to say to GLBTQ teens. You'll find biography, biographical stories, and memoirs, as well as interviews and collections of personal essays written by GLBTQ authors.

Andronik, Catherine.

Wildly Romantic: The English Romantic Poets: The Mad, the Bad, and the Dangerous. **Holt, 2007.** **S**

Many teens probably have the idea that the Romantic poets were a bunch of stodgy guys in uncomfortable ruffles, and that couldn't be further from the truth. The Romantic poets were the badly behaved rock stars of their time, involved with drug use and indiscriminate sex. Adronik also addresses their political views. Although this selection strays from the usual informative nonfiction titles for and about GLBTQ teens, readers may be excited to discover that the poets they study in English class felt many of the same things they did and weren't much different from today's celebrities. (G)

Keywords: biography

Bechdel, Alison.

🎞 *Fun Home: A Family Tragicomic.* **Houghton Mifflin, 2006.** **S** **A/YA**

This critically acclaimed work is Bechdel's memoir of growing up in a world of sexual confusion and dysfunctional parents. Her literary and melodramatic father, who manages a funeral home and likes to think of himself as an aristocrat, is emotionally distant and barely in the closet. Her mother, a former actress, acts out the role of a happy spouse. Daughter Bechdel works at restoring the family's nineteenth-century home and maintaining a façade of familial normalcy as long as she can. Lesbian teens may already know Bechdel's award-winning *Dykes to Watch Out For* comic strip, but even those who are unfamiliar with her work will find this popular book funny and insightful. (G, L)

Awards/honors: GGNT

Keywords: graphic novel; memoir

Boyer, David.

🎞 *Kings and Queens: Queers at the Prom.* **Soft Skull Press, 2004.** **S**

Prom is stressful enough for the average high school student, between dates, dresses, flowers, and the like, but throw in being gay, lesbian, bisexual, or transgendered, and prom stress takes on a whole new meaning. This collection of twenty-three stories spans more than seventy years of proms. These prom attendees attend a diverse array of schools, from Harvey Milk High School to the Bronx High School, and they speak not only about their own experiences, but about their high school environments and lives after the prom. The format is visually appealing, with photographs and collages, and a glossary is included. (GLBTQ)

Awards/honors: PPYA

Keywords: personal essays; prom

Boylan, Jennifer Finney.

She's Not There: A Life in Two Genders. **Broadway, 2004.** **A/YA**

Boylan, a novelist for adults, tells her story of living life as a woman in a man's body. Jennifer began her life as James Finney Boylan. Although she always struggled with her gender identity, she lived as a man for forty years, even marrying and fathering children. Boylan chronicles her transition from male to female, both physical (including hormone therapy and gender reassignment surgery) and emotional, using humor and honesty. Her narrative is more colloquial than academic, making the book easily accessible for the average reader. (T)

Keywords: memoir

Jennings, Kevin.

Mama's Boy, Preacher's Son: A Memoir of Growing Up, Coming Out, and Changing America's Schools. **Beacon Press, 2006.** **A/YA**

Growing up poor in a culture that considered bullying a normal part of masculinity and homosexuality an abomination was disheartening for Jennings. Because he was neither strong nor athletic, he became a self-described "mama's boy." By following his mother's example of determination (his mother, who was not highly educated but was gifted at math, became the manager of a local McDonald's), Jennings excelled in school and eventually earned admission to Harvard. When he began his teaching career, his sexuality became a cause of inner turmoil, and he eventually went on to create the Gay, Lesbian and Straight Education Network (GLSEN). (G)

Keywords: memoir

Planned Parenthood of Toronto.

🎋 *Hear Me Out! True Stories of Teens Educating and Confronting Homophobia.* **Second Story Press, 2005.** **S**

Members of the volunteer organization T.E.A.C.H. (Teens Educating and Confronting Homophobia) share stories of discovering and living with their sexual identity. The twenty stories come from people of diverse racial and socioeconomic backgrounds. The theme tying the stories together is the need for freedom to express who they are without fear of being harmed or seen as ill, and to be tolerated, even respected. Teachers and youth workers can benefit from this collection, too, using it to spark discussion. Includes contributor bios. (GLBTQ)

Awards/honors: PPYA

Keywords: personal essays

Scholinski, Daphne.

The Last Time I Wore a Dress. **Riverhead, 1997.** **A/YA**

When she was young, neither Scholinski's family nor her friends understood her. Her father beat her and she acted up at school, leading her counselors to send her to a mental health facility for three years at the age of fifteen. While there, she was diagnosed with "Gender Identity Disorder," and a million dollars of insurance money was spent "fixing" her disorder, including things like makeup lessons and encouragement to make physical contact with male staff members. At the end of three years she was discharged, now expected to make her way in the world as a proper woman . . . but without a high school education. (T)

Keywords: memoir

Sutton, Roger.

Hearing Us Out: Voices from the Gay and Lesbian Community. **Little, Brown, 1994.** **S** **A/YA**

Sutton, currently the editor-in-chief of *Horn Book*, interviewed fifteen distinct individuals, including three teens, who tell fifteen very different stories about their sexuality and how they are affected by it. The interviewees include people who are politically active, some who are raising adopted minority children in same-gender-parent families, and a teen who ended up dropping out of high school and pursuing a GED because after he came out, his fellow students harassed him and the faculty and staff did nothing about it. The introduction, in which Sutton describes his own sexuality and the prevalence of stereotypes about the GLBT community, is especially enlightening. (G, L)

Keywords: interviews

Trachtenberg, Robert.

🏵 *When I Knew.* **Regan Books, 2005.** **A/YA**

Eighty people from varying career fields and social backgrounds each contributed a story on the topic of how they knew they were gay. Some of the names may be familiar to teens, including *Law & Order: Special Victims Unit* star B. D. Wong. Many of the anecdotes contain observations about how a person's sexual realization was influenced by popular culture. The stories take many different tones, from funny to heartbreaking, increasing the book's audience. Each entry is short, just a page or two, and accompanied by a visual component such as a cartoon or picture. (G, L)

Awards/honors: PPYA

Keywords: personal essays

Winick, Judd.

🏵 *Pedro and Me.* **Holt, 2000.** **S** **A/YA**

Judd Winick met Pedro Zamora when they were both cast on MTV's *The Real World: San Francisco.* Openly gay Zamora, originally from Miami, became sexually active at an early age and was living with HIV. Originally Winick was conflicted about his thoughts about Zamora, who was at the time a renowned AIDS educator. Over time the two became friends and maintained a relationship long after leaving the show, and when Zamora died at age twenty-two, Winick, a cartoonist, took over Zamora's mission of AIDS education. (G, QP)

Awards/honors: BBYA

Keywords: AIDS; graphic novel; memoir

Wright, Kai.

Drifting Toward Love: Black, brown, gay and coming of age on the streets of New York. **Beacon Press, 2008.** **S** **A/YA**

Manny, Julius, and Carlos are all from poor areas of New York City and its boroughs, and each is struggling with his sexuality in his own way. Manny engages in unsafe sex, Julius faces homelessness and poverty in his quest to find love, and Carlos must balance his sexuality with his role as his family's patriarch. Wright entwines the boys' stories with a history of gays and people of color in New York City, profiling the rise of safe havens for young gays and lesbians in a voice reminiscent of Jonathan Kozol. (G)

Keywords: history; profiles; safe havens

Collections, Short Stories, Poetry, Essays, and Photo Essays

Short, powerful poems, stories, and essays can reach the heart of a reader just as easily as a novel. In these collections, readers get the chance to sample the writing of many different authors and see their real-world experiences in forming their own identities or, in the case of straight writers, their relationships with their GLBTQ peers. These collections are all nonfiction; fiction collections appear in previous chapters.

de la Cruz, Melissa, and Tom Dolby, eds.

Girls Who Like Boys Who Like Boys: True Tales of Love, Lust, and Friendship between Straight Women and Gay Men. **Dutton, 2007. A/YA**

Using their own friendship to form the concept of the book, de la Cruz and Dolby invited well-known authors for teens and adults, including Cecil Castellucci, David Levithan, Brian Sloan, and Wendy Mass, to contribute essays about the unique relationships between straight women and their gay male friends. The five sections of the book cover different aspects: group dynamics; one-on-one adult friendships; romances from the funny to the sad to the misguided; adolescent friendships, which focus on dare-to-be-different girls and their gay male friends; and familial relationships (both parents and children). (G)

Keywords: essays; relationships

Garden, Nancy.

Hear Us Out! Lesbian and Gay Stories of Struggle, Progress, and Hope, 1950 to the Present. **Farrar, Straus & Giroux, 2007. J S**

Both fiction and nonfiction works offer a wide variety of viewpoints in this volume. Each fiction story chronicles an important moment in the life of a GLBT teen. These stories are accompanied by essays and accounts of important moments in GLBT history, such as the Stonewall Riots. Rather than presenting a wholly optimistic or wholly pessimistic point of view, the stories vary in theme and tone, reflecting the attitudes of both society at the time the story takes place and the narrators. The common thread through the stories is the need for acceptance and tolerance from all, at any time. (G, L)

Keywords: essays; short stories

Heron, Ann, ed.

Two Teenagers in Twenty: Writings by Gay and Lesbian Youth. **(Paperback reprint). Alyson Publications, 1995. J S**

This collection of personal essays from gay and lesbian teens from all over the United States and Canada provides an update to the author's *One Teenager in Ten* (Alyson Publications, 1983). Twenty-four of the essays are reprints from the earlier edition, and nineteen are new. Some of the essays come from teens who found acceptance from their loved ones after coming out, but more than one chronicles the ostracism and oppression gay teens face, including being forced to see a psychiatrist and attempted suicide. The diverse range of experiences will appeal to many readers. (G, L)

Keywords: personal essays

Levithan, David, and Billy Merrell, eds.

The Full Spectrum. **Knopf, 2006.** S

In cooperation with GLSEN, the editors collected forty essays from young writers (none with established careers as YA authors) to present personal stories of sexuality and identity. The stories take all forms, from letters to diary entries to a photo essay, and address a wide range of the identity issues GLBTQ teens face, including questioning their sexuality, dealing with family members who don't accept them, viewing their sexuality alongside their religions, and their first romances. The personal, highly emotional writing will appeal to any teen looking for honest stories about coming out. (GLBTQ)

Keywords: personal essays

Mastoon, Adam.

The Shared Heart: Portraits and Stories Celebrating Lesbian, Gay, and Bisexual Young People. **HarperCollins, 1997.** J S

Mastoon is not a writer but a professional photographer, and he brings his photography skills to this work that captures forty gay, lesbian, and bisexual teens. His subjects are all older teens and young adults, and they are Caucasian, Latino, African American; from rural as well as urban environments; and with a wide range of personal interests, from arts to sports. Each black-and-white photograph is accompanied by a testimonial from its subject about the ways in which sexuality affects his or her life. The subjects' honesty and diversity resonates with many teens. (GLBT)

Awards/honors: BBYA

Keywords: photo essays

Merrell, Billy.

Talking in the Dark. **Push, 2003.** S

In free verse poetry, Merrell, now twenty-four, writes a memoir of his parents' divorce when he was seven and his realization of his homosexuality. Merrell writes with wisdom about his relationships with his parents, especially the aspect of those relationships that revolved around his sexuality. His comfort in his sexuality may offer solace to some readers; he writes that it is a part of him that he has always known. Other topics he covers, all discussed with sophistication, include death, friendships, and family relations. (G)

Keywords: memoirs; verse

Peterson, John, and Mark Bedogne, eds.

A Face in the Crowd: Expressions of Gay Life in America. **Prospect Publishing, 2002.** A/YA

Pictures, including one by celebrity and fashion photographer David LaChapelle, capture "a day in the life" of a diverse gay, lesbian, bisexual, and transgender population. The photos reveal that there is no one stereotype that fits GLBT people. His subjects represent a wide variety of socio-economic backgrounds, and they also live their lives with joy, honesty, and sometimes even fear. Photos are accompanied by biographies of prominent GLBT people and capture important events in GLBT history. The photo essay format of this book may be especially appealing to reluctant readers. (GLBT)

Keywords: biography; photo essay

Reed, Rita.

Growing Up Gay: The Sorrows and Joys of Gay and Lesbian Adolescence. **W.W. Norton, 1997.** J S

Reed, a photographer for the Minneapolis *Star Tribune*, created this photo essay book about two teens, Amy Grahn and Jamie Nabozny because she believed that Amy and Jamie could benefit from knowing about each other's struggle with sexuality and love. Amy and Jamie have many of the same relationship experiences their straight peers do, including falling in love for the first time. Their lives are complicated by society's prejudices against their sexualities, but they have a strong foundation at home of supportive, loving families. Includes a list of literary and technological resources for teens, including social organizations. (G, L)

Keywords: photo essays

Sonnie, Amy, ed.

Revolutionary Voices. **Alyson Publications, 2000.** J S

Teens will identify with the contributors to this work, who range in age from fourteen to twenty-six and write poems and essays about their experiences with sexuality and gender identity using humor, honesty, and pathos. The collection includes amateur as well as established writers, such as Audre Lorde. In many cases sexuality is discussed as being only one aspect of the writer's personality and background, next to ethnicity and race. Includes glossary of GLBTQ terms, including non-gender-specific pronouns, and a list of resources for GLBTQ youth (hotlines, etc.). (GLBTQ)

Keywords: essays; poetry

Informational and How-To

Every librarian wants to help his or her patrons find accurate information from reputable sources. Every librarian also knows that typing "gay" into a search engine is asking for information disaster. With these books, young adult readers can get answers to many of their questions on sexual health and identity and gay and lesbian history. Although not every book in this section was written with the teen reader in mind, most have friendly, knowledgeable, approachable voices.

Alsenas, Linas.

Gay America: Struggle for Equality. **Amulet, 2008.** **J** **S**

This detailed yet readable work covers more than a hundred years of GLBTQ American history. It is illustrated with photographs and portraits of important people in gay and lesbian history, including Eleanor Roosevelt and James Baldwin, and features both high and low points in the fight for equality. The book is structured to read like a story, but it can also serve as a starting point for students interested in learning more about queer theory and history. (G, L)

Keywords: equal rights; history

Bass, Ellen.

Free Your Mind: The Book for Gay, Lesbian, and Bisexual Youth—And Their Allies. **HarperCollins, 1996.** **M** **J** **S**

The author's thoughtful voice will appeal to a wide of audience of gay, lesbian, and questioning youth and their families and friends. This book is designed to make everyone feel empowered about his or her or another's sexuality and achieve understanding and tolerance. It is divided into six sections, on self-discovery, friends and lovers (including tips for safer sex), family, school (which offers advice on how to deal with different kinds of discrimination), spirituality, and community. Included are photos, graphs, interviews with prominent gays and lesbians, and resources such as videos, social services, and hotlines. (G, L, B)

Keywords: personal growth

Helminiak, Daniel.

What the Bible Really Says About Homosexuality. **Alamo Square Distributors, 2000.** **A/YA**

Teens with both scholarly and spiritual interest in the Bible may enjoy Helminiak's work. He cites troublesome translations rather than an outright, stated belief that homosexuality is wrong as the problem with religious views of homosexuality. However, he does not say definitely whether the Bible takes a stance on homosexuality, which may lead to frustration for readers looking for black-and-white answers. (G, L)

Keywords: Bible

Hogan, Steve, and Lee Hudson.

Completely Queer: The Gay and Lesbian Encyclopedia. **Holt, 1998. S** **A/YA**

There's a little bit of everything that queer and questioning teens may want to know in this book, from brief profiles of gay people in history and popular culture to word definitions, professional organizations, and headings such as "activism," "gender," "drugs," and "AIDS." (G, L)

Keywords: encyclopedia

Huegel, Kelly.

🎖 *GLBTQ: The Survival Guide for Queer and Questioning Teens.* **Free Spirit Publishing, 2003.** **J** **S**

> More than just a life guide for GLBTQ teens, this volume addresses social and personal issues queer teens, as well as their straight friends and family, encounter. Topics include homophobia, religion, coming out, dealing with parents who are not accepting of the teen's sexuality, and harassment. Autobiographical anecdotes and pictures of smiling, multicultural teens are interspersed with Huegel's straightforward, down-to-earth text, reassuring queer teens that they are not alone. Although it touches on sexual health issues for GLBTQ teens, it is not primarily an anatomy and sexuality guide. Includes Web and print resources. (GLBTQ)

> **Awards/honors:** PPYA

> **Keywords:** personal growth

Loukas, Keith.

🎖 *Ask Dr. Keith: Candid Answers to Queer Questions.* **Whitecap Books, 2004.** **A/YA**

> Loukas, who holds a degree in medicine, started an advice show much like *Loveline* (started at KROQ in Los Angeles; ran on MTV 1996–2000), answering sex, health, and relationship questions from the Toronto GLBT community. His forum became a place where GLBTQ people could ask questions about the physical and emotional sides of sex and sexual identity. With fun facts and straightforward information, Dr. Keith answers questions about HIV/AIDS, relationships, coming out, sex, sexuality, and physiology. Although teens are not his primary audience, his advice can help any GLBTQ person of any age. (GLBTQ)

> **Awards/honors:** PPYA

> **Keywords:** health; personal growth; sexuality,

Marcus, Eric.

🎖 *Is It a Choice? Answers to the Most Frequently Asked Questions about Gay and Lesbian People.* **3rd ed. HarperSanFrancisco, 2005.** **A/YA**

> Som e of the questions Marcus has answered over the course of his life include Why do gay people hold hands in public? and What's it like for gay people who hide their sexual orientation?, but the question he is asked most often is, Is it a choice? Using that question as a starting point, Marcus compiled hundreds of questions on sex, family, work, socializing, and other topics relating to GLBTQ people and answered them honestly and without lots of overwhelming medical details. This is a book that straight as well as gay readers will find enlightening. (GLBTQ)

> **Awards/honors:** PPYA

> **Keywords:** personal growth

Pardes, Bronwen.

Doing It Right: Making Smart, Safe, and Satisfying Choices About Sex. **Simon Pulse, 2007.** 🟦 🟦

> Pardes holds a graduate degree in human sexuality and is currently an HIV counselor in New York. Known as "The Sex Lady," she writes from years of experience teaching middle and high school sex education. The safer sex practices she covers include oral, anal, and vaginal sex. One chapter covers questioning and alternate sexualities, and another discusses what it means to be transgender and intersex. The Q&As in those sections include answers to questions many GLBTQ teens have, such as How do gay people have sex? and If I have a sexual dream or fantasy about someone of the same sex, does that mean I'm gay? (GLBTQ)
>
> **Keywords:** health; sexuality

Pollack, Rachel, and Cheryl Schwartz.

The Journey Out: A Guide for and About Lesbian, Gay, and Bisexual Teens. **Viking, 1995.** 🟦 🟦

> Whether teens are questioning their sexuality or are already sure of their sexual orientation, they can gain much from this volume, which includes testimonials from gay and lesbian teens, advice on coming out, how to handle harassment, the place of homosexuality in religion, maintaining self-esteem, and sexual health advice. The language is conversational yet informative, reassuring GLBQ teens that they are not alone in their feelings. Although some of the resources (community services, etc.) may be outdated, the advice is still strong and current, encouraging teens to act responsibly and take their sexuality seriously. (G, L, B, Q)
>
> **Keywords:** coming out; essays; testimonial

Rich, Jason.

Growing Up Gay in America: Informative and Practical Advice for Teen Guys Questioning Their Sexuality and Growing Up Gay. **Franklin Street Books, 2002.** 🟦 🟦

> Rich's most important message to gay guys is that no matter what happens, they are not alone. Readers are reassured that there is more to coming out than just standing up and saying, "I'm gay"; they have to consider the potential reactions and feelings of family and friends, and how their sexuality fits or doesn't fit their personal spirituality. Topics include but are not limited to sex, building a support system, coming out, dealing with relatives, and relationships and dating. (G)
>
> **Keywords:** coming out; dating; family; relationships; sexuality

St. Stephen's Community House.

The Little Black Book for Girlz: A Book on Healthy Sexuality. **Annick Press, 2006.** 🟦 🟦

> Even though this book is not strictly aimed at lesbian teens, tips for safer lesbian sex are included and treated as being equally as important as tips for safer, more enjoyable heterosexual sex. The writers, who are teenage girls themselves, encourage healthy sexuality and knowledge about the functions of the female body regardless of sexual preference. Chapters include but are not limited to "Relationships," "Periods," "Sex," "STIs," and "Sexual Assault." Interspersed in

the educational text are funny cartoons, photos, and essays (some anonymous) about love, desire, sex, and relationships. (L)

Keywords: health; sexuality

The Little Black Book for Guys: Guys Talk about Sex. **Annick Press, 2008.**
Pop culture meets sexual health. Many mysteries of male sexuality are ex-
plained, including penis size, safer sex, contraception, sexually transmitted
diseases, and a chapter called "Sex: Do Ya Really Need It?" The up-front
language matches the tone of *The Little Black Book for Girlz,* encouraging
frank discussions of sexual health while respecting that teens like their information in sound bytes. Raw language was not a fear of the authors of this
book. The collection also includes personal essays, poems, and art with a
"to one guy from another" tone.

Keywords: health; sexuality

Winfield, Cynthia.

Gender Identity: The Ultimate Teen Guide. **It Happened to Me series. Scarecrow Press, 2007.** **S**
Rather than dealing specifically with gay and lesbian identities, this book
focuses on transgender and intersex people. Comics by Erin Lindsey, cre-
ator of *Venus Envy*, a Webcomic centered around a transsexual teen, are in-
terspersed within the text. The text, although sometimes dry and academic,
provides a strong foundation in transgender and intersex research and terminology. Despite the disparity between text and comics, this is a book recommended for most library collections because there are currently no other
books that address these issues and are specifically aimed at teens. Includes
a glossary, teen testimonials, further reading, and photographs. (T)

Keywords: comics; intersex; testimonial; transgender; transsexual

Chapter 7

GLBTQ Collection Development

In 2009, the latest trend in GLBTQ teen literature was incidental gay and lesbian characters. Once relegated to the role of problem-causers or car crash victims, gay and lesbian characters now pass through many young adult books as a part of the fabric of the narrator's life. They don't play into the plot of the book or even matter that much to the main character. More important, the main character doesn't think that being gay or lesbian is anything out of the ordinary. One example of this is Justine Larbalestier's *How to Ditch Your Fairy* (Bloomsbury, 2008). At one point, the (female) main character, Charlie, makes a casual mention of a boy and "his boyfriend." Nothing else is ever mentioned about this character, not even his name.

So if he doesn't even warrant a name, how can he be important?

Gay and lesbian characters who are acknowledged as existing but ultimately have no bearing on the story represent something significant: their acceptance. To Charlie, a person's sexuality is just part of who he or she is, end of discussion. She doesn't fixate on it. More important, Larbalestier acknowledges by writing in gay characters of no consequence that many teens are tolerant of their peers' diverse sexualities. Although not everyone in the real world or in literature is tolerant, this shift in YA literature toward making GLBTQ characters as normal as everyone else helps the genre progress. Keep in mind that treating these GLBTQ characters as inconsequential doesn't mean that the author sees them as undeserving of their own story; it only means that they aren't germane to the main character's story. GLBTQ characters have been around YA literature for nearly fifty years, and their stories aren't going anywhere.

Why is this a collection development concern? In some communities, any mention of GLBTQ characters might be unacceptable, even if the characters only appear in one sentence. These incidental characters probably won't be mentioned in professional reviews, either, because professional reviews have strict word limits that may not accommodate the mention of incidental characters.

It comes as no surprise to any librarian that books with GLBTQ content for teens are often the target of censors. In 2007 Maureen Johnson's *The Bermudez Triangle*, in which two girls fall in love, was banned in the Bartlesville Public Schools in Bartlesville, Oklahoma. Johnson reproduced the content of a letter from a parent who objected to the book's availability in her blog.[1] Part of the letter states that topics such as homosexuality do not belong in a school library, and that this book lacks moral fiber:

> Johnson reported at a YA authors' panel at the New Jersey
> Library Association conference in 2009 that the librarian
> who informed her of the book challenge stepped down from
> her job.

This letter shows one thing that is often misunderstood by those who object to GLBTQ content in YA literature: Sex, sexuality, and romance are all distinctly different things. Although this may seem obvious to those involved in YA literature collection development, patrons do not always understand the distinction. *The Bermudez Triangle* is tame in terms of sex; there is a kiss between two girls, but no sexual activity beyond that. A book in which two boys hold hands is not automatically more adult in nature than a book in which a boy and a girl have sex. What patrons such as the parent who wrote the letter to Maureen Johnson show is their objection to sexuality and the idea that teens can and do question theirs. Johnson is not the only author to encounter this kind of challenge to her books.

In 2009 the West Bend Community Memorial Public Library in West Bend, Wisconsin,[2] encountered a complaint about its "Out of the Closet" booklist, which included fiction and nonfiction for and about gay teens. The complainant went to great lengths to stress that she was not a censor; she did not ask the library to remove the books from the shelves. Instead, she wanted to move books with GLBTQ content from the YA section to the adult shelves, even if these books were written for and marketed to teens and purchased for the library's teen collection. She also requested that the library purchase "pro-heterosexual" books and books by and about "ex-gays," or people who were gay but are now straight due to efforts in prayer and faith. This issue divided the town of West Bend and spawned two popular blogs on opposite sides: *WISSUP: Wisconsin Speaks Up* at wissup.blogspot.com, and *West Bend Parents for Free Speech* at westbendparentsforfreespeech.webs.com. A meeting to discuss the books, which was open to the public, ended up being canceled because so many people showed up that the fire department had to clear out the meeting space. Ultimately, library director Michael Tyree and the library board decided to keep the books in the teen section. To learn more about the controversy in West Bend, try the following links:

> "Wisconsin Library Challenge Heats Up":
> http://www.schoollibraryjournal.com/article/CA6656504.html?industryid
> =47055

> "West Bend Library Stands up for LGBT Literature":
> http://www.examiner.com/x-13512-Milwaukee-Gay-Community-Examiner~
> y2009m7d22-West-Bend-library-stands-up-for-LGBT-literature

> "West Bend Library Book Meeting":
> http://www.wisn.com/news/19020024/detail.html

The controversy in West Bend was not the only challenge to GLBTQ teen literature that made headlines in 2009. In the wake of the West Bend decision, a group called the Christian Civil Liberties Union filed a claim against the West Bend Library, asking for financial compensation they claim they deserve due to Francesca Lia Block's *Baby Be-Bop* (Joanna Cotler Books, 1995) being on the library's shelves. Four members of the CCLU petitioned the library for permission to burn the book. They claimed that *Baby Be-Bop* promoted hate speech because of its inclusion of words like "faggot" and "nigger."

For more information about the would-be burning of *Baby Be-Bop*, try these links:

> "Library Book Riles small Wisconsin Town":
> http://abcnews.go.com/US/story?id=7874866&page=1

> "Milwaukee Group Seeks Fiery Alternative to Materials Challenge":
> http://www.ala.org/ala/alonline/currentnews/newsarchive/2009/june2009/westbendbabybebop060309.cfm

> "A Teen Book Burns at the Stake" (this article includes some quotes from Francesca Lia Block):
> http://www.salon.com/books/feature/2009/06/16/francesca_lia_block/index.html

To provide readers' advisory to those who want to read GLBTQ books, it is essential to have a collection that includes them. Although collection development is technically not a part of readers' advisory, several aspects of it, including reading reviews, analyzing the community, and deselecting books at the end of their useful lives, all help broaden one's knowledge to use in performing readers' advisory.

While considering collecting GLBTQ YA novels, you may hear some of the following statements:

> "I don't know any gay, lesbian, bisexual, or transgender teens."

> "Gay teens don't come into my library."

> "No one's ever asked me for a 'gay book!'"

> "Books with gay characters belong in the adult section of a library, not the young adult section." Alternately, "Our children shouldn't be exposed to these lifestyles."

> "We can't have these books in school libraries."

> "I'm straight, therefore I don't know anything about these books, and I can't collect them for the library, much less recommend them."

> "I buy these books, but they don't circulate."

These are some common protests against adding GLBTQ teen books to a library collection, and on the surface, they look like legitimate protests. In the face of facts, however, they don't hold up.

First, although you might not know any gay teens, that does not mean they don't exist in your library population. Exactly what percentage of the population is gay is unknown, but a study by the Human Rights Campaign estimates that gay people make up 5 percent of the population. One widely held estimate is that about 5 to 10 percent of the population is exclusively gay, and many more people fall on a spectrum between exclusively gay and exclusively straight. Working with this 10 percent, ask yourself this: If 10 percent of your town's population were Hispanic, or Orthodox Jewish, wouldn't you make sure you had books that feature Hispanic or Orthodox Jewish characters or had Hispanic or Orthodox

Jewish themes? Gay teens deserve books in which they can see themselves, just like any minority segment of the population. Libraries play an important role in marketing ideas of tolerance and diversity; by their very nature they are one of the few institutions that welcome all people and ideas. Having books with GLBTQ characters enhances a library's collection by making it more diverse and more reflective of the world. Consider this quote from Arthur A. Levine, the head of Scholastic's Arthur A. Levine Books and J.K. Rowling's editor:

> Ten percent of the children's book readership, at least, will grow up to be gay or lesbian. . . . Wouldn't it be nice if their first exposure to the idea that there are gay people in the world isn't when they're teenagers—so when little Johnny falls in love with that really cute, brainy boy in his computer class, he's grown up with the idea that it's not unusual and there's nothing wrong with that.[3]

Levine notes that a larger percentage of readers will eventually know someone who is gay or lesbian and questions why there are not more books for children and teens that normalize the lives of gay and lesbian people, stating, "When you think about it that way, it's even more of a mystery why there aren't more of these books."

Second, it is impossible to tell a person's sexuality just by looking at, or even by talking to, that person. Although there are gay and lesbian stereotypes, just as there are stereotypes of any group (including librarians!), it is ludicrous to think that you can apply them to your patrons. Straight women can have short hair and wear motorcycle boots. Straight men often enjoy Broadway shows. Gay men work in construction and play professional sports, and lesbian women can be models and homemakers. Sitting at a reference desk, you can never tell before a patron opens his or her mouth what that patron will ask. Senior citizens do not always want medical or genealogical information. High school students don't always need help with their homework. It is impossible to see a person's interests or reference needs without talking to him or her, and it is impossible to see a person's sexuality without doing the same. In this same vein, remember that although your teen patron might not tell you he or she is gay, that doesn't mean he or she isn't. A girl looking for books with lesbian main characters may very well be a lesbian or believe she is one, but she could be looking for books for a friend or for a school project. She might be curious about what a lesbian relationship is like. Perhaps a friend told her that the book was really good, and she trusts her friend's taste in literature. Not all adolescents, straight, gay, or otherwise, are wholly comfortable with their sexuality. Their bodies and brains are changing, and their questions about identity are endless.

Remember: You don't know whether your teen patron is gay, and there's a chance he or she doesn't know, either. Many people do not fully realize their sexuality until they are in their twenties, thirties, or even later. What you can do is make high-quality, popular books about GLBTQ teens available and recommend them when appropriate. You can do your best to ensure that all patrons are treated equally regardless of their sexuality or gender.

The third point, regarding the demand, or lack thereof, for "gay books" (ignoring, of course, the fact that books do not have a sexuality), is tied closely to the second point. Because so many teens are uncomfortable with their sexuality, they may not want to walk up to you, a virtual stranger, and specifically ask about books for and about gay teens. Even if you believe there is no demand for books about GLBTQ teens and your collection does not currently have any, consider buying one or two popular, recent titles, just to have them available. If you learn via a "dusty book" report that the books are not circulating even if you promote them, you can always weed them. If you find that your GLBTQ books are being stolen, look at this as a positive: It means someone, for better or worse, knows they are there. In addition, by linking to reliable, informative Web sites with bibliographies of GLBTQ teen literature, you can do passive readers' advisory for teens who might feel more comfortable exploring their sexuality anonymously on the Internet. Look through the sites for titles that recur and consider investing in those.

Think of popular genres in fiction: realistic, mystery, romance, science fiction, fantasy, etc. Do you have demands for these genres? GLBTQ books fit into many of them; there are GLBTQ romances, fantasies, and realistic fiction. When buying GLBTQ books in these genres, it may help you to think about your larger genre needs first and the GLBTQ factor second.

Fourth, when purchasing books for a YA section and questioning their place in the library, GLBTQ books should be judged by the same standard as any other genre. When deciding placement of a book based on sexual content, ask yourself: If the characters in this book were straight, where would this book be placed in the library? GLBTQ novels, like all others, should be placed in the library according to their content and vocabulary. What do reviews have to say about the placement of these books in libraries? Are they specifically written with a YA audience in mind, or adults? Patrons may question you about the appropriateness of "exposing children to alternative lifestyles." Look at it this way: There is no one right way to live, just as there is no one right book that belongs in all libraries. Chances are that at least one of your young patrons is living "that lifestyle" with two same-sex parents, or has family friends or relatives who are same-sex parents. If you keep your collection diverse and buy books based on community needs and professional reviews, your collection should serve your patrons regardless of their political, social, or religious views.

School libraries often have much stricter collection development policies than public libraries have; school librarians must be more restrictive with what they purchase for their libraries in terms of content. However, if you buy for a school library, or are a public librarian advising a school librarian, don't automatically write off GLBTQ books or resign them to the category of "issue" books. If you're looking for additions to a summer reading list, consider the actions of the characters rather than the fact that there is GLBTQ content. Judge the book on the basis of what happens onstage in the book. Is there kissing? Hand-holding? Intercourse? What would keep this book off the shelves if the characters were straight? Remember when working with summer reading lists that homosexuality is not necessarily a problem that teens must "deal with" or "cope with." For many teens, as seen in some selections in the "Friends" and "Family" sections in chapter 2, homosexuality is simply a normal part of their lives. To only include books in which sexuality and/or gender is a problem tells GLBTQ students that their lives are problematic, not normal, and not deserving of inclusion. Following are some "clean" (meaning nothing more physical than kissing happens between same-sex partners and there is little to no physical violence) books with GLBTQ central characters:

The Misfits by James Howe

Totally Joe by James Howe

The Bermudez Triangle by Maureen Johnson

Absolutely, Positively Not by David LaRochelle

Dramarama by E. Lockhart (Although the characters, who are high school seniors, do discuss sex, none of it is on-screen.)

M or F? by Lisa Papademetriou and Chris Tebbetts

Luna by Julie Anne Peters

So Hard to Say by Alex Sanchez

Regarding your own sexuality, being straight does not diminish your ability to read reviews in professional journals, ask questions of collection development experts about the genre, or buy high-quality books about and for GLBTQ teens. Collection development is not about your home life or personal beliefs; it's about serving your population. You may not be African American or male, or have divorced parents, but you can collect books about African Americans, boys, and children with divorced parents. When doing readers' advisory it is most important that you keep an open mind and do your best to listen to your patrons' needs, rather than actually experience what goes on in the books. Patrons ask your opinions during readers' advisory because they trust your knowledge of literature, not because they are sure that your personal views align with theirs 100 percent.

Once you have purchased quality GLBTQ books for your collection, you may find they don't circulate as well as some of your other fiction. This is not necessarily a good reason for weeding them, because depending on the nature of your community, your patrons may worry about facing persecution if they are found in possession of a GLBTQ book. A book that doesn't circulate is not necessarily sitting on the shelf and collecting dust, either. Because so many GLBTQ teens deal with uncertainty or fear regarding their sexuality, they may feel more comfortable taking the book off your shelves and finding a quiet corner of the library in which to read it, rather than checking it out and risking being seen with it.

The best way to increase the likelihood of your books being read is to buy titles that are not only high quality but are also popular and relevant. Some well-known authors whose names often come up when professionals discuss GLBTQ books are listed in the appendix; these are the authors you should look to first.

Where You Can Find Quality GLBTQ Books

Your town may have a gay and lesbian bookstore; if it does, talk to the shop's proprietor(s) about some outstanding and popular titles for teens. But if your library is out in the middle of nowhere, don't despair! GLBTQ teen novels are regularly reviewed in *Booklist, VOYA, Kirkus, School Library Journal,* and other professional publications. You'll also find a list of Web sites in the appendix that provide synopses of and bibliographic information for GLBTQ books. Usually you can purchase these books through major distributors or bookstores, although a handful may only be available directly from their publishers.

How You Can Raise Awareness of GLBTQ Books in the Library's Collection

Even though GLBTQ teens might not come forward and ask for these books, you can subtly let them know that you have them in your collection by doing any or all of the following:

- When you create book displays around a genre or topic, see what GLBTQ books you have that will fit under the other genre. You could include Perry Moore's *Hero* in a display of fantasy and science fiction novels, or Bill Konigsberg's *Out of the Pocket* in a display of books about sports.

- You can give the books their own display or readers' advisory list in June, which is Gay and Lesbian Pride Month.

- Include GLBTQ books in any booktalking sessions you may give, assuming that their content fits the theme of the session.

- During readers' advisory sessions, offer GLBTQ books as appropriate. You will have to know your audience, but because readers' advisory is generally done along genre lines, you may want to consider adding GLBTQ books with the content a reader seeks to his or her list of recommended titles.

- If you keep a regular display of new books, keep GLBTQ titles with them as appropriate, rather than sending them straight to the regular collection.

- Make use of Web 2.0 technologies. If you maintain a readers' advisory wiki, update it with GLBTQ titles. If your library has a teen blog, write a blog entry on a GLBTQ book of your choice.

Things to Look for in the Books You Want to Add to Your Collection

Developing a GLBTQ collection for teens doesn't mean running out to buy every book with a GLBQ character or theme. Instead, look for books with the following characteristics:

- There is a lack of death and disease in GLBTQ characters. If you judge a GLBTQ YA novel by no other criteria, take note of what happens to a GLBTQ character in regards to diseases (sexually transmitted or not) and death. For years heterosexual couples that had sex in YA literature were punished for their acts by contracting diseases or getting pregnant, and homosexual characters died in offstage car wrecks. Thankfully the publishing trend is moving away from punishing GLBTQ characters and toward tolerance and acceptance, but this is something all collection developers should watch for when considering the purchase of GLBTQ books.

- If you want your realistic fiction to fully mirror the lives of today's teens, look for books that incorporate a wide variety of reactions to a character's coming out. The sad truth is that many gay teens who come out will experience what Holland goes through in Julie Anne Peters's *Keeping You a Secret*: Her mother throws her out of the house and she has to depend on friends for help. However, many teens will also experience love and acceptance from friends and family, as in David LaRochelle's *Absolutely, Positively Not*. Just as GLBTQ teens should not be punished for their existence by death or disease, they should not all be punished in a library's collection by becoming outcasts and losing their friends and family.

- The general rule to keep in mind about gay teens is that there is no one way to be a "gay teen." After all, not all jocks are dumb, and not all science enthusiasts wear pocket protectors and watch *Star Trek*. GLBTQ teens are just as diverse in their interests and personalities as their straight peers, and your collection should reflect that. When looking at your GLBTQ books, check to see how diverse the characters are in terms of background, interests, hometown, and goals in life. Gay boys should not always pursue stereotypically "feminine" interests, and lesbian girls should not always have short hair and eschew dresses.

- Nonfiction books on sexual health and relationships should acknowledge the existence of gay, lesbian, and transgender teens. Ideally, they should discuss safer sex practices for teens of all sexual orientations and encourage healthy relationships between same-sex couples. Homosexuality has not been labeled a disease since the 1970s, and your nonfiction collection should reflect this. When reading reviews of books geared toward teen sexual health, see if the review mentions whether same-sex relationships and transgender teens are discussed, and if so, what the book says about them. Quality contemporary sexual health books *should* cover same- as well as opposite-gender relationship concerns.

What to Do If Your GLBTQ Books Are Challenged

Challenges to GLBTQ materials should be handled just like challenges to any other book. This may seem an obvious answer, but in an era where information and misinformation can spread so quickly around communities, it is important to keep a clear, professional head in response to book challenges. Even if you work in a liberal community, you must always be prepared to encounter a book challenge, especially considering that *And Tango Makes Three* by Peter Parnell and Justin Richardson (Simon & Schuster, 2005), the story of two male penguins who hatch and raise a daughter, was the most banned book of 2006,[4] 2007,[5] and 2008.[6] *And Tango Makes Three* is not aimed at a young adult audience, but its homosexual themes made it a target for book banners.

Young adult books, despite being aimed at an older audience, are not immune to objections based on homosexual content, even if it is innocuous. Three of the remaining nine most-challenged books are YA and were banned for homosexual content: *The Perks of Being a Wallflower* by Stephen Chbosky (MTV Books, 1999), *Athletic Shorts* by Chris Crutcher (Harper, 1991), and the <u>Gossip Girl</u> series by Cecily Von Ziegesar (Little, Brown, 2002). In each of these books, homosexuality is presented as a normal part of the everyday lives of the characters. The main characters, their parents, and their friends are gay, and no one is punished for it. This may be the driving force in some book challenges; beyond the simple fact that GLBTQ characters are present in a work of literature for young adults, homosexuality is presented as a normal part of life. The acceptance of homosexuality as normal is something you should strive to include in your YA collection, even if it only occurs in one book. As mentioned previously, Generations Y and M are used to seeing gays and lesbians in the media. They know that gay people exist, and that they work and live just the same as straight people. When your YA books are challenged, the normalcy of GLBTQ teens' existence is challenged as well.

Following are some preemptive strikes you can take against challenges to your GLBTQ books:

- Have a solid collection development policy for all materials, not just books with GLBTQ content or YA books (or graphic novels, or any other special collection in the library). If your library doesn't have a collection development policy, consider developing one. It can benefit all library staff as well as patrons. A sampling of library collection development policies can be found at Acqweb (http://www.acqweb.org/cd_policy.html).

- Do not attempt to confront the patron who wants to remove your GLBTQ materials and change his or her mind at the reference desk. Instead, hand him or her a form and say as calmly as possible, "Please fill out this form, return it to me, and someone will contact you in the near future." This may not be easy! Librarians are often very passionate about defending their collections against would-be censors, and it would be easy to start a screaming match over a book, but it is important that you maintain a professional demeanor at all times. On the flip side, maybe you don't believe that GLBTQ books belong in the YA section. If this is the case, it is just as inappropriate to tell the patron that you agree with his or her stance on your collection as it is to immediately rise up and defend a book without consulting your collection development policy.

- Staff training for both professionals and paraprofessionals is key to ensuring that patron objections are handled seriously. It is possible that members of your own staff feel uncomfortable handling materials with GLBTQ content. To give both patrons and the library staff a chance to have their say regarding a GLBTQ book's place on the shelf, staff should be trained to react to a patron's complaint. Training, workshops, and role-playing can give staff the tools they need to handle patrons irate about a book's content. Not every complaint will lead to a challenge, but proper support for the staff is key. Remind your staff that when they are at work their primary job has to be equal service for all patrons, and that patrons with complaints are best referred to the library director.

- In addition to your collection development policy, have a form available for people who want to contest a book's place on your shelves. This form should be the same for any book in the library and should include questions such as, "What content do you object to?" "What do you suggest should be done with this book?" and most important, "Have you read this book in its entirety?" A sample form is available at http://skyways.lib.ks.us/KLA/intellectual_freedom/reconsideration.html#request.

- The strongest defenses you will have when you make a case for a title's place on your shelves are professional reviews. Teen-written reviews and customer reviews on sites like Amazon can be useful if you want to gauge the reactions of a book's target audience, but when it comes to deciding whether a book will be a worthwhile addition to your collection, professional reviews from industry publications are seen as the most reliable resource for librarians and booksellers. As soon as someone challenges your materials, start collecting professional reviews to take to any meetings you may have about the book's future in your collection.

- The first people you talk to about the challenge should not be your blog audience, the ACLU, the Human Rights Campaign, AS IF (Authors Supporting Intellectual Freedom), or the ALA Office for Intellectual Freedom. They should be your supervisor and/or your director. If you expect your patrons to follow certain steps when they ask that a book be removed from your collection, it is your duty to your library and to your profession to follow the steps required of you.

Collection development is never an exact science, but using these tips and acquiring some of the books mentioned in this guide should get you well on the way to serving the GLBTQ readership.

Core List of GLBTQ YA Fiction

If You Can Buy Only Five Books, Purchase These

Annie on My Mind by Nancy Garden

Boy Meets Boy by David Levithan

Luna by Julie Anne Peters

Empress of the World by Sara Ryan

Rainbow Boys by Alex Sanchez

If You Can Buy Ten Books, Add These

Am I Blue? Coming Out from the Silence edited by Marion Dane Bauer

The Perks of Being a Wallflower by Stephen Chbosky

My Heartbeat by Garret Freymann-Weyr

The Misfits by James Howe

Hard Love by Ellen Wittlinger

If You Can Buy Fifteen Books, Add These

Down to the Bone by Mayra Lazara Dole

The Vast Fields of Ordinary by Nick Burd

Geography Club by Brent Hartinger

Freak Show by James St. James

Parrotfish by Ellen Wittlinger

When Buying Nonfiction, the Following Should Be a Priority

Note that these books are annotated in chapter 6.

Gay America: Struggle for Equality by Linas Alsenas

GLBTQ: The Survival Guide for Queer and Questioning Teens by Kelly Huegel

The Full Spectrum: A New Generation of Writing About Gay, Lesbian, Bisexual, Transgender, Questioning, and Other Identities edited by David Levithan and Billy Merrell

Although the following are sold as two separate books, unless your patronage is entirely female or entirely male, it's a good idea to buy them together.

Is It a Choice? Answers to the Most Frequently Asked Questions About Gay & Lesbian People by Eric Marcus

The Little Black Book for Guys: Guys Talk About Sex and The Little Black Book for Girlz by St. Stephen's Community House.

Endnotes

1. maureenjohnson.blogspot.com/2007/04/i-am-very-dangerous-person.html

2. www.west-bendlibrary.org

3. Stephen Frank, *Battles Rage Over Children's Books with Gay Themes* (AfterElton.com, June 25, 2007).

4. www.ala.org/ala/issuesadvocacy/banned/frequentlychallenged/21st centurychallenged/2006/index.cfm

5. www.ala.org/ala/issuesadvocacy/banned/frequentlychallenged/21st centurychallenged/2007/index.cfm

6. www.ala.org/ala/issuesadvocacy/banned/frequentlychallenged/21st centurychallenged/2008/index.cfm

Appendix

GLBTQ Web Sites and Professional Resources

Use these resources for personal development or point teens to them. Parents, teachers, and other professionals who work with teenagers may find these Web sites useful for their own reading and knowledge development. Some of the sites and books include fiction booklists with a GLBTQ focus. Please note that because this is a reader's advisory guide, not a guide to library or social services, these resources focus more on books and reading than on activism, health, or social issues.

Web Sites

Organizations and Education

The American Library Association Office of Intellectual Freedom
ala.org/oif

Established in 1967, the ALA OIF "is charged with implementing ALA policies concerning the concept of intellectual freedom as embodied in the Library Bill of Rights, the Association's basic policy on free access to libraries and library materials. The goal of the office is to educate librarians and the general public about the nature and importance of intellectual freedom in libraries." The ALA OIF is responsible for compiling statistics on banned books and assisting libraries whose collections are challenged or censored.

AS IF: Authors Support Intellectual Freedom
Asifnews.blogspot.com

AS IF began when St. Andrew's Episcopal School in Austin, Texas, turned down a large donation. The donation was offered on the condition that Annie Proulx's short story "Brokeback Mountain," which is the story of a romance between two cowboys, be removed from the optional reading list for twelfth graders. A group of YA authors, impressed by the school's refusal of the donation, donated signed copies of their books to the school library. Since then, the group has chronicled efforts of censorship and raised awareness about intellectual freedom for both teens and adults.

The Comic Book Legal Defense Fund

www.cbldf.org

The Comic Book Legal Defense Fund does not exist solely to oppose censorship of graphic novels and comics with GLBTQ content, but GLBTQ content is one of the things the organization strives to protect. The CBLDF contributes to the representation of publishing industry professionals, including booksellers, who enter legal battles to defend the selling or display of graphic works.

The Gay, Lesbian, Bisexual, and Transgendered Roundtable of the American Library Association

www.ala.org/ala/glbtrt/welcomeglbtround.htm

From the Web page: "The GLBTRT is a unit of the American Library Association. The GLBTRT was founded in 1970 as the Task Force on Gay Liberation. We are the nation's first gay, lesbian, bisexual and transgender professional organization." Members of this roundtable receive the GLBTRT newsletter, which includes book reviews and news on the roundtable's efforts to increase awareness and quality of library services to GLBTQ people.

glbtqYAwriters at Yahoo! Groups

groups.yahoo.com/group/glbtqYAwriters/

Even though this list was created for writers of GLBTQ YA literature, all advocates of the genre are welcome to join and participate in the discussions. Librarians may find it useful as a readers' advisory tool.

GLSEN: The Gay, Lesbian, and Straight Education Network

glsen.org

This organization, a cosponsor of No Name-Calling Week, educates the public about GLBTQ issues through events like the Day of Silence and supporting gay–straight alliances (GSAs).

Human Rights Campaign

hrc.org

This is a research and advocacy organization dedicated to "working to achieve gay, lesbian, bisexual and transgender equality."

No Name-Calling Week

www.nonamecallingweek.org/cgi-bin/iowa/home.html

This project sprang from James Howe's book *The Misfits* and encourages schools across America to have one week every year that is free of name-calling and derogatory remarks, not just about sexual orientation, but about race, class, disabilities, and more.

PFLAG: Parents and Friends of Lesbians and Gays

www.pflag.org.

PFLAG maintains chapters in all fifty states, and the Web site is a wealth of resources for supporting gay and lesbian friends and family members. The three main divisions of the site are "Advocacy," which includes links on bullying and comprehensive sex education; "Education," which discusses

PFLAG's current social education and political projects; and "Support," where users can find a local PFLAG chapter. PFLAG has a division for supporting transgender people, too: TNET can be found at www.pflag.org/Support_for_Transpeople.1082.0.html.

Blogs, Booklists, and Pop Culture

AfterEllen

www.afterellen.com

Pop culture enthusiasts looking for more substance than just pictures of the hottest celebrities will enjoy this news and social networking site that focuses on lesbian and bisexual women in the news and media. Features include television and movie recaps and reviews.

AfterElton

www.afterelton.com

This is the companion site to AfterEllen, only its focus is on gay men in the media.

GLBTQ Month Archive at YA Books Central

www.yabookscentral.com/cfusion/index.cfm?fuseAction=home

GLBT YA Books Central, a blog dedicated to the discussion of YA literature, hosted a month focusing on books with GLBTQ content. Both authors and publishers contributed to the archive, offering interviews and books for review.

I'm Here, I'm Queer, What the Hell Do I Read?

www.leewind.org/

Fantasy author Lee Wind writes YA fantasy with GLBTQ characters, and GLBTQ people in books, media, and pop culture are the focus of his blog. His blogroll includes a continually updated list of gay and lesbian YA literature.

Oz GLBT YA Books (started at Justine Larbalestier's blog)

justinelarbalestier.com/blog/?p=685

As of the publication of this book, this list of GLBTQ books published for teens in Australia is neither complete nor annotated, but it is an ongoing project that will have a place at the Centre for Youth Literature at the State Library of Victoria, Australia (www.slv.vic.gov.au/about/centreforyouthliterature/youthlit.html). Although these Australian titles are often difficult to find in the United States and are not reviewed by major U.S. publications, if you have the financial resources you may want to consider adding one or two of the most popular titles to your collection.

PinkBooks

www.pinkbooks.com

PinkBooks focuses on lists of GLBTQ books for children, teens, and parents. Be forewarned that the site has not been updated since 2006, but it can still serve as a way for you to check your collection and see what older or rare books your collection may house.

Queer YA

daisyporter.org/queerya

Maintainer Daisy Porter is a librarian, book reviewer, and expert on YA literature. She presents and writes on the subject of GLBTQ literature and presents useful, journal-style reviews on her blog. One of her outstanding features is her coverage of small press books, which are not reviewed in professional journals as often as their peers from large presses.

The Rainbow List @ MySpace

myspace.com/rainbow_list

Rainbow List @ the ALA GLBTRT blog

blogs.ala.org/glbtrt.php?cat=441

The Rainbow List is a project of the ALA's GLBT Roundtable, started in 2007, with the first list appearing in 2008. They research and recommend books with GLBTQ content for children, teens, and adults.

The Trevor Project

thetrevorproject.org

The Trevor Project works to maintain suicide prevention hotlines specifically for GLBTQ youth. It offers advice to both GLBTQ teens and their straight friends and loved ones, including tips on recognizing the signs of suicidal thoughts and where to get help locally.

Worth the Trip

worththetrip.wordpress.com

Children's literature expert K. T. Horning blogs about GLBTQ books and their coverage in the media.

Awards and Booklists

The Lambda Literary Award

www.lambdaliterary.org

Sponsored by the Lambda Literary Foundation, this award is given to GLBTQ-focused books from many genres, for many audiences. From the Web site: "Our mission is to celebrate LGBT literature and provide resources for writers, readers, booksellers, publishers, and librarians – the whole literary community . . . . The Lambda Literary Awards seek to recognize excellence in the field of lesbian, gay, bisexual, and transgender literature. Each year, over 80 judges—writers, booksellers, librarians, journalists—assess the entries in more than 20 categories."

NYPL Books for the Teen Age

This list often includes a GLBTQ-specific booklist, and books with GBLTQ main or secondary characters often show up on other themed lists that are part of Books for the Teen Age.

The Stonewall Book Award

The Stonewall, given by the Gay, Lesbian, Bisexual, and Transgendered Roundtable of the American Library Association, is "the first and most enduring award for GLBT books." It is awarded annually to English-language works.

YALSA awards and lists

ala.org/yalsa

These include but are not limited to Best Books for Young Adults, Great Graphic Novels for Teens, the Michael L. Printz Award, Popular Paperbacks for Young Adults, and Quick Picks for Reluctant Young Adult Readers. None of these awards is specifically given for books with GLBTQ content, but GLBTQ content almost always appears in books that appear on these lists.

Books

Bosman, Ellen, and John P. Bradford. *Gay Lesbian, Bisexual and Transgendered Literature: A Genre Guide.* **Edited by Robert B. Ridinger. <u>Genreflecting Advisory Series</u>. Libraries Unlimited, 2008.**

This guide to adult GLBT literature for adults covers both fiction and nonfiction, organized into lists that reflect popular genres and reading interests. Although not thorough in its coverage of teen titles, titles that appeal to teens are identified as such.

Cart, Michael, and Christine Jenkins. *The Heart Has its Reasons: Young Adult Literature with Gay/Lesbian/Queer Content, 1969–2004.* **Scarecrow Press, 2006.**

literature experts Cart and Jenkins take an academic, in-depth look at the history and progression of GLBTQ characters in teen literature over a thirty-five-year span. Rather than analyze every book with GLBTQ content, the authors look to outstanding (for good or bad) works for examples of changes in the portrayal of GLBTQ teens. This highly readable volume is recommended for all literature professionals interested in learning more about the genre. An index, appendices, and charts are included. YA

Day, Frances Ann. *Lesbian and Gay Voices: An Annotated Bibliography and Guide to Literature for Children and Young Adults.* **Greenwood Press, 2000.**

Aimed at librarians, teachers, and parents, this guide covers not only books for teens, but books for younger children as well. Parents and professionals both can use this book, which includes author profiles and a list of GLBTQ resources such as a calendar of days important to the GLBT community, publications, hotlines, and annotations of nearly 300 books. It is divided into sections covering picture books, fiction, nonfiction, short stories, biographies, and autobiographies. Although this book is a few years old, librarians and teachers can still use it for collection checks and recommendations about titles they may already have in their libraries.

Martin, Hillias J., and James R. Murdock. *Serving Lesbian, Gay, Bisexual, Transgender, and Questioning Teens: A How-to-Do-It Manual for Librarians.* **Neal-Schuman Publishers, 2007.**

If you are interested in "selling" your GLBTQ YA collection and developing programs and services aimed at GLBTQ teens, this book is a must-read. Librarians Martin and Murdock offer tips, including booklists, on how to develop a strong component of GLBTQ books for your collection (including lists of suggested books), marketing them to readers in need, and programming for this special population. Whether your community is more liberal or more conservative, you will find clues on how to be inclusive regarding books about GLBTQ teens.

Authors to Know

Many authors are named in this book, but this is a quick list of popular authors who have written more than one young adult book focusing on GLBTQ characters. If your collection is lacking in GLBTQ materials, these are the authors you'll want to look for first. All have received excellent review of their books, and their books have been named to some of the YALSA lists mentioned previously.

- Rachel Cohn, www.rachelcohn.com/
- Nancy Garden, www.nancygarden.com/
- Brent Hartinger, www.brenthartinger.com
- Ron Koertge. Although he has no official Web site, a brief biography and some of his suggested reading are available at www.teenreads.com/features/2002-koertge-ron.asp
- David Levithan, www.davidlevithan.com/
- E. Lockhart, www.theboyfriendlist.com/
- Julie Anne Peters, www.julieannepeters.com/
- Tamora Pierce, www.tamora-pierce.com/
- Alex Sanchez, www.alexsanchez.com/
- Ellen Wittlinger, www.ellenwittlinger.com/
- Jacqueline Woodson, www.jacquelinewoodson.com/

Author/Title Index

Subject Index

Keyword Index